AT
PERSONAL
RISK

Boundary Violations in Professional-Client Relationships

Marilyn R. Peterson

W. W. Norton & Company • NEW YORK • LONDON

The text of this book is composed in Janson. Composition by Bytheway Typesetting Services, Inc. Book Manufacturing by Haddon Craftsmen, Inc. Book design by Justine Burkat Trubey

Library of Congress Cataloging-in-Publication Data

Peterson, Marilyn R.
    At personal risk : boundary violations in professional-client relationships / Marilyn R. Peterson.
        p. cm.
    ISBN 0-393-70138-7
    1. Professional ethics.   I. Title.
BJ1725.P48   1992
174–dc20   91-46343   CIP

W. W. Norton & Company, Inc. 500 Fifth Avenue, New York, N.Y. 10110
W. W. Norton & Company, Ltd. 10 Coptic Street, London WC1A 1PU

8 9 0

A NORTON PROFESSIONAL BOOK

To Norton, who, while I wrote
this book, became a nurturer and my friend

ACKNOWLEDGMENTS

WHEN I REFLECT ON HOW THIS BOOK came to be, I find myself moved by how many lives are mirrored in the pages that follow. I did not write this book alone. Rather, I became a conduit to express the truths we all know but sometimes fail to heed. I feel privileged. I therefore want to acknowledge my community and express my gratitude to those who stood with me and made this project possible.

Foremost, I respect and am profoundly grateful to Rene Schwartz for her love and wisdom, for helping me to find my own voice, and for her belief in this book and in me.

My special thanks goes to the professionals in my community and to those individuals whose life experiences I describe in this book. I admire their bravery in exposing their stories. I am greatly affected by the sincerity of their struggle to heal rather than take revenge, the preciousness of their contributions, and the weight of the responsibility I feel to honor and respect their words.

I want to acknowledge those therapists who shared their concerns about their own and others' tendencies to cross the boundary with clients and who referred friends and clients to be interviewed for the book.

I am appreciative of the efforts of the members of my consultation group, who were supportive and who validated and enhanced what I had surmised about the universality of the professional-client relationship.

I am grateful to Kathleen Michels for her rigorous (though gentle) and unrelenting focus and for her genius in editing and shaping my voice.

I acknowledge my family of origin, who taught me about power in vulnerable relationships, the myriad ways it is used to control others, the proclivity to misuse it, and the damage that can result.

And I am deeply grateful to Jan Feris, my cousin, who held and allowed me to discover the health in my family and who inspired optimism in me and led me to my own spiritual wellspring by continuously sharing with me her faith and her own process.

I admire and thank my daughter, Stephanie Armour, whose courage to write truthfully about what she saw as a journalist and expose herself to controversy served as a model for me.

I want to recognize Minna Shapiro, my early teacher and mentor, who taught me to take risks and to make the covert overt and who challenged me to find the courage to be who I am.

I also recognize Marianne Walters, who clarified the significance of empowering others, helped me to appreciate the importance of maintaining the relational connection, and instilled in me the need to keep context as the central filter for processing relational dynamics.

I am greatly indebted to Marilyn Mason, who was an early enthusiast for the credibility of the ideas expressed in this book. She pushed me to go beyond what I thought I knew, guided me through unknown waters, and provided the warmth, encouragement, and safety net that made my trip much less fearful.

I am thankful to Peg Thompson for the constancy of her availability and for her personal and professional sensitivity to my needs. She challenged my intellectual cautiousness and generously shared from her own experience as she joined with me in wrestling over the theoretical concepts presented here.

And I am deeply indebted to Ann Varco, my lifelong friend, who knows where I come from and where I am now, and gives me the love and permission to play and discover all of what lies ahead.

CONTENTS

AT
PERSONAL
RISK

INTRODUCTION

FOR CENTURIES, THE CONDUCT of society's most trusted servants was deemed above reproach. Physicians, attorneys, clerics, and teachers were assumed to be paragons of wisdom, morality, and excellence. Today, such blind faith is fast disappearing from the landscape. No longer are the professions of law, education, medicine, religion, and psychotherapy exempt from the critical scrutiny of a better-informed and increasingly skeptical – and litigious – public. For example, the Ethics Committee of the American Psychological Association (1988) reported that between 1985 and 1987 the number of clients intending to file complaints against their psychologists increased by 76%.

Boundary violations with clients* are not a recent development or unusual occurrence. Indeed, 5% to 13% of professionals in the mental health disciplines, medicine, and religion have engaged in sexual contact

---

*This generic term refers to patients, parishioners, students, and other consumers who receive service from members of the professions discussed here.

with their clients, patients, and parishioners (Schoener, 1989). Moreover, 10% to 30% of female college students are sexually harassed by academic faculty (Robertson, Dyer, and Campbell, 1985). What is different now from in the past is that a more vocal public has pushed professional malfeasance to the forefront of its attention. As a result, the media is reporting, with ever greater frequency, instances of insurance fraud, medical negligence, and mismanagement of client funds, as well as sexual misconduct. Professionals in practice today have good reason to be frightened.

While many individual professionals are worried about this trend, the hierarchy of professions has been reluctant or even unwilling to explore the magnitude of the problem. For example, Lawrence Dubin (1988), former chairman of the Michigan Attorney Grievance Committee, reported that the Family Law Section of the State Bar of Michigan denied him permission to publish a questionnaire to collect data about divorce attorneys' sexual behavior with clients. Similarly, Dr. Nanatte Gartrell (Gartrell, Olarte, and Herman, 1986), a member of the American Psychiatric Association Committee on Women, disclosed that she was denied monetary as well as other forms of support when she sought permission to conduct a national survey of the American Psychiatric Association's membership regarding psychiatrist-patient sexual conduct. Unfortunately, such reluctance to get at the truth has left both clients and professionals ill-equipped to protect themselves.

The decision to turn away from the problem has allowed it to fester and has added to the consequences imposed on professionals. For example, insurance payments to victims have resulted in a significant increase in the cost of malpractice premiums for all professions. In addition to the financial impact, professionals are experiencing the results of their colleagues' transgressions in the form of more stringent codes of ethics, codes of conduct, and other professional regulations that have curtailed or restricted certain behaviors and have made all of us more watchful about what we do with clients.

CONTEXT VERSUS CONTENT

Professionals tend to identify and describe boundary violations in terms of content. This approach is potentially hazardous, as it provides no early warning system short of the actual event to alert us professionals to impending trouble. Moreover, when violations are defined on the basis of content, those that are seemingly less egregious and visible tend to be ignored, normalized, or dismissed as not serious. Finally, and perhaps most important, placing the primary emphasis on the content of the violation eclipses the more fundamental injury, the injury to the core of the professional-client relationship itself.

In this book, I move beyond content to explore boundary violations through the lens of the professional-client relationship. From this frame of reference, boundary violations involve a *process* of disconnection that occurs within the context of the relationship. This exposure expands the spectrum of behaviors that are hurtful to clients and widens and deepens our perspective so that we can view the issue more comprehensively.

Moreover, instead of treating the fields of law, medicine, religion, education, and psychotherapy as separate entities, I emphasize the dynamics of the professional-client association that transcend the domain of each of the morally and ethically based disciplines, that is, those that oblige a professional to place the needs of others ahead of his or her own.

Chapter 1 is presented from the client's perspective. It examines the professional's anointment as society's trusted servant. In the client's eyes, the core of the connection with a trusted servant has a spiritual dimension. Boundary violations occur in part because our society is increasingly minimizing this dimension. The professional's obligation to make the client's needs primary is reframed as a covenant and traced through the regulatory codes of each profession.

Chapter 2 describes the power differential that gives structure to the professional-client relationship. The sources of the professional's power and inherent limits on the client's self-determination make the disparity in the relationship more apparent. Boundaries are defined as limits that protect the space between the professional's power and the client's vulnerability.

Chapter 3 is presented from the professional's perspective. It examines the professional's struggle with his or her power. Boundary violations grow out of the professional's attempts to either equalize the power differential or discount the relationship. Such attempts alter the boundaries that protect the primacy of the client's needs.

Chapter 4 describes the four characteristics of a boundary violation and the series of relational changes that damage the professional-client bond. The interaction between these four elements makes a boundary violation a process, not an end product.

Chapter 5 recounts the damage done to a victimized client. Without the involved professional's help to sort out what happened between them, the client is left to struggle with the injury alone. His or her solo attempts to master the pain are, for the most part, misdirected and undertaken at great personal cost.

Chapter 6 defines what professionals and clients need to do both independently and together to heal the wound to the relationship. Clients are faced with grieving what they have lost and with what they must do to return the responsibility for the violation to the professional. For their part, professionals are confronted with their shame, terror, and proclivity to assume a self-protective posture.

Chapter 7 is written from my personal perspective. I believe it is possible to heal a wound to the professional-client relationship, but certain psychological, professional, and societal obstacles impede such healing. At this juncture, the future of relational healing looks bleak, because our faith in what we can do together is steadily being undermined and destroyed by the society in which we live.

THE STORY BEHIND THE BOOK

I wrote this book to help professionals—of which I am one—better understand the enormity of our impact on clients. I also wanted to share the ethical tools that have helped me first to understand and then to work with what happens between me and my clients in hopes that you can gain from my experience. It is written out of my concern for the clients we inadvertently hurt. It is written out of my disappointment with our formal training, which teaches us how to use sophisticated techniques but gives us little or no guidance about how to appreciate and deal with the professional-client relationship. It is written out of my compassion for all of us who, for the most part, strive to do the right thing. Finally, it is written out of my fear that the defensive approach we are taking to address our mistakes can only leave us isolated and afraid and further erode the professional-client connection.

The foundation for this book was laid in my childhood. I learned early from my parents, both of whom were classical musicians, that music and the demands of a musician's life could be used to justify their placing their professional needs ahead of the needs of their children. Concerts, rehearsals, and daily practicing always had the highest priority. Because our needs just seemed to get in the way of things that were more important, my parents viewed them as a sign of weakness or pathology and effectively suppressed them by idealizing their mission in life. To sacrifice who you were for something as lofty as music was deemed by them to be a measure of strength.

My parents, of course, were not "responsible" for this state of affairs. They espoused the myth that to make a living they had no choice but to respond to the dictates of their calling. Since they were "sacrificing" for us, my brothers and I were expected to keep our needs to a minimum. We sacrificed for them so that they could sacrifice themselves to their profession.

Early in my career, my history allowed me to recognize clients who had been exploited by professionals. The admiration and power given the professional because of his or her superior talent, skill, wisdom, or artistry felt similar to the homage I paid my parents for their specialness as musicians. When clients contended that the specialness of the professional's job or abilities justified or excused his or her misconduct, I found the distortion familiar. When clients asserted that compromising themselves was a necessary trade-off for the valuable service the professional performed, I readily recalled the logic I had used to suppress my own feelings.

Just as I had, these clients questioned their worthiness and the validity of their needs. They tried to hide their needs from the professional or ministered to the professional's needs, so that they could get what they needed in return. They normalized the professional's behavior, declaring that he or she could not help what had happened, that it was beyond his or her control, or that it was the result of the arduousness of the task or the hardships involved in the performance of his or her duties. They believed that the professional was really trying to take good care of them. Most important, they were afraid to speak the truth for fear it might anger the professional and possibly affect the service they needed or their safety in the relationship.

In my years as a social worker and psychotherapist, I have counseled many such clients. In working with them, I found that the experiences of individual clients were remarkably parallel and transcended the artificial distinctions that otherwise mark and separate the morally and ethically based professions. I saw that a change in the content of the violation or the field of practice did not alter the constancy of the interactional process all my clients reported or the profound sense of betrayal they all felt. I began to recognize the universality of the professional-client relationship and the generic principles that transcend the specifics of each profession.

My decision to help clients violated by professionals was not made hastily or without trepidation. It came about because their pain touched my own. It came about because I finally surrendered to hearing the part of their story I wanted to cancel out: Members of my professional family were hurting the same people I was trying to help. It came about because my own awareness of this truth led me to the realization that I could help clients recognize what had happened to them.

Being that truthful about my colleagues was extremely painful. Because they were part of me and I was part of them, I could not write them off as I could other offenders. As a result, I found myself drawn to helping other mental health professionals who were struggling with setting appropriate boundaries for themselves. For five years, I supervised a group of clinicians who were brave enough to let me see their conflicts and the damage they had done to their clients, themselves, and their agencies. As I was able to help my colleagues find the courage to face what had happened, acknowledge their responsibility, and repair the damage, I found the relief I sought from the pain of my own clients' experiences. I know today that my ability to help them and other professionals grew out of the empathy I had for my mother who, although she was a part of the system, continuously struggled "to get it right."

I have long believed that professional mistakes are common. We all make them. Unfortunately, our demand for perfection and the shame we experience block us from acknowledging and learning from them. Therefore, we must learn both to hold ourselves accountable and to accept the reality of our human fallibility.

Even though I had advocated this position for years, I was not prepared for the hell I experienced when I discovered that I, too, had done things that hurt my clients. Although these situations were not sexual or otherwise egregious and I did what I could to minimize and/or repair the damage, I had absolutely no tolerance for my own misconduct. Acknowledging what I had done (more than once) was painful, but being forced—because of my reaction to myself—to see my own arrogance and self-delusion was excruciating. I truly believed that I of all people should know better. I truly believed that my education and experience had equipped me to be other than an ordinary person. I truly believed that I possessed the mechanisms that would alert me to my blind spots. Today, I remain deeply grateful to my professional friends who lovingly challenged me with the truth of my own philosophy and helped me to be humble and accept myself in a core way as being no different from anyone else. My personal suffering and self-condemnation irrevocably deepened my compassion for other professionals and the agony they feel when they face the monsters that lurk within.

RED HERRINGS TO SIDESTEP

Readers of this book face a difficult challenge. As professionals, you will naturally try to distance yourselves from the complexity and discomfort of the subject matter by defining violations as stories of victims and villains. To move beyond a pious "we" or an awful "they," however, it is essential that you simultaneously experience the world of the client and the world of the professional. Not making this shift is apt to leave you stuck either in your shame and self-hatred or in a defensive (and ultimately self-destructive) position that keeps you afraid of what you keep hidden within. If you are able, however difficult, to balance both realities, you will inoculate yourself against your own grandiosity or sense of mission and find yourself better able to respond when you hurt a client. In remaining open to this process, you will probably be awakened to past or current situations that are painful and arouse shame. It is important to be gentle with yourself, accept your humanity, and not close down.

Some readers, I expect, will question the merits of this book because of an aversion to the term "spirituality" and the tendency to equate it with religion. This is understandable, since many professionals who have been trained to be rational, scientific, and objective carry a built-in prohibition against using concepts and terms that deal with the metaphysical dimensions of life. For me, however, spirituality has nothing to do with organized religion. Instead, I view it as our reverence for life and our activities in behalf of all that is life-affirming. Since the essence of the professional-client relationship is built on this concept, the spiritual issue is core to understanding the trust that is damaged by boundary violations and the healing that is needed.

Some readers will no doubt question this book because of its feminist underpinnings—that is, it is built on a relational model. I ask professionals to place the professional-client relationship first, view the client's needs as ascendant, make decisions within the context of that association, and risk themselves to stay in-right-relation (Friedman, 1960) to the client. I suggest that the problems we encounter grow out of our attempts to divorce ourselves from this relational mandate. In my opinion, the highest value should be placed on the ethic of care, accountability, and connection.

Readers who believe my position is too feminist or who are in search of quick answers will feel weighed down by the attention I give to the emotional aspects of the professional-client association and the heavy emphasis I place on the need to be both relational and responsible. In contrast, readers who believe my position is not feminist enough may want to discount the book because of my position on power and the reality of the power differential. If you cling to the belief that mutuality rests on needing to be equal or the same or that acknowledging your power is oppressive or harmful to clients, you will miss the reality of the potential for professionals' power to enhance the relational connection and empower clients. In either instance, my hope is that all of you will move toward a more complex and comprehensive view of your responsibility for what takes place in the professional-client relationship.

THE ISSUE OF COURAGE

Writing this book has been an act of courage. I have tried to shed light on the lack of awareness on the part of professionals that is hurting clients and professionals alike and to name what is true as I see it. The ideas I espouse are ultimately political and controversial. They threaten the status quo and illicit shame from other professionals, whose reactions have ranged from support to confusion to attacks on my credibility.

The people I interviewed for this book had courage too. Instead of merely describing the boundary violation, they carefully explored and, at times, reexperienced the pain of their trauma so that they could teach us who we are to them. Their thoughts and experiences are an integral part of the text.

As readers and as professionals, you, too, will need courage – to listen, to reflect, to try new behaviors, to grow. I hope you read this book from deep within yourself and risk being vulnerable. Your giving of yourself in this way makes the endeavor we share mutual, honest, and possible.

I

THE ANOINTMENT
OF PROFESSIONALS

A T THE CORE OF HUMAN EXISTENCE are our needs for physical and psychological survival, belonging to community, love from another human being, a sense of self-worth, and actualization of our creative being (Maslow, 1968). From time immemorial, we have constructed mechanisms for responding to these basic needs. In some societies, a mystical and transcendent shaman is anointed keeper of the specialized knowledge required to meet these needs. Western society, with its emphasis on rationality, has allocated the responsibility instead to specific professional groups. The professionals in these groups are respected and acknowledged as vital to our individual and collective welfare. According them an elevated status reflects the importance of our needs and grants them the authority necessary for performing their jobs. We are conditioned to comply with their directives; we are taught that our cooperation is necessary if we are to receive fully from them.

To comply, though, we have to believe that professionals will place our needs ahead of their own. This assumed agreement is more than a legalistic contract. To place our faith in the unknown requires a level of commitment that raises the relationship to the level of a covenant of professional promise and personal trust. As a society, we have no difficulty recognizing the secular aspect of professionals' expertise. However, acknowledging the more spiritual element of our faith in professionals' abilities makes us uncomfortable. (In the context used here, the word *spiritual* does not mean religiosity; rather, it refers to the universality of life—the life we connect to in ourselves and in each other so that we can give ourselves more fully to what life asks of us. Likewise, the word *faith* does not refer to religiosity; rather, it means giving ourselves fully to that which we cannot control.) Since we tend to accept only what is rational, knowable, and seeable, we place these more transcendent and elusive concepts out of our awareness. Yet, keeping them covert is dangerous. When we limit our vision only to the more secular aspects of the connection, we minimize the full dimensions of the relationship and thereby pave the way for boundary violations.

THE SHAMAN AND THE PROFESSIONAL

The archetype of the shaman addresses more specifically the suppressed dimension of our connection with professionals. In a world controlled by gods and spirits, belief in the shaman's abilities to garner the forces of the world beyond to protect the community is critical for survival. We do not realize that we act out of a similar place when we entrust professionals with our care. We, too, have to make a giant leap of faith in professionals' abilities to guide us through unknown, mystifying, and sometimes dangerous waters.

The Role of the Shaman

The shaman's function is to heal the mind, body, and spirit. "Called" to attend to the physical, emotional, social, and spiritual needs of his or her community, the shaman stands as a wise and unusually gifted specialist.

Sometimes a healer, ceremonialist, judge, or sacred politician, the shaman is a pivotal figure who defends against disease, sterility, disaster, death, and the world of darkness.

The role of the shaman is to garner and wield power in order to protect the welfare of the community. By undergoing an ecstatic and dissociative experience that includes suffering, death, and resurrection, the shaman receives the inner powers necessary for helping others. Knowledge from traditional teachings and training from ancestral or older shamans provides the shaman with the specialized and secret language that allows him or her to access spirits and to decipher the specific mysteries of nature. With these tools, the shaman "can go below and above because he has already been there. The danger of losing his way in these forbidden regions is still great; but sanctified by his initiation and furnished with his guardian spirits, the shaman is the only human being able to challenge the danger and venture into a mystical geography" (Eliade, 1964, p. 182).

While the shaman is an extraordinarily powerful figure, his or her strength is combined with the power of belief. The shaman convinces others to believe in his or her energy to effect a cure or to follow his or her direction. "This sense of conviction or confidence is the shaman's greatest asset because by it he convinces others of the truth and their joint belief creates a joint reality" (King, 1987, pp. 201–202). Indeed, the shaman's importance springs from the relationship between the shaman and the community. Considered indispensable to the maintenance of the social and metaphysical equilibrium, the shaman is accorded prestige, honor, and respect by the community. As the antidemonic champion, the shaman stands apart, assuring the community of his or her guardian presence and assuaging the danger that lurks outside (Eliade, 1964).

The Role of the Professional

Contemporary professionals are secular shamans who preserve, protect, and treat our minds, our bodies, our souls, and our relationships with each other. The shaman's tasks have been parceled out to five disciplines: medicine, law, religion, teaching, and psychotherapy. Each has its own unique function and social responsibility. While we may have modernized the shaman's functions, our core needs remain unchanged. And we still need to trust those who can help us feel safer, stronger, and less alone. "We really want somebody to take care of part of our lives. We want somebody to stand between us and the terror of the universe." This quote from a professional identifies the mythical hope that resides within and echoes through us all. At its highest level, each profession holds a transcendent vision of its purpose that reflects the importance of our needs and the importance of each professional's function in our lives.

Physicians

Physicians attend to our physical well-being. They are trained to minimize illness and keep us alive. From conception to death, they monitor our health. We come to understand that our bodies are our instruments, that physical incapacity affects our psychological outlook, and that the quality of our survival is directly linked to our care. Mortality rates measure the health of our nation and broadcast to others the weakness or strength of our citizenry. Living within the vulnerable vessel of our physical selves, we all share a common journey and a common fate. Our longevity and the quality of our days pivot on the mainspring of our physical health.

Attorneys

Lawyers attend to the rights and obligations that enable us to live together in an orderly fashion. At their best, they protect the ideals and principles on which our society is founded. They engineer the parameters of what is allowed and what is not, constructing and adhering to a set of rules that reflects our inherent sense of what is right and equitable. Attorneys articulate our passions rationally. Going beyond an eye for an eye and a tooth for a tooth, attorneys navigate for us the territory that both defines what justice means and determines what is fair. Theoretically, they protect us from harm. As the object of premeditated, negligent, or inadvertent injury, we call on these emissaries to fight for our human liberties and claim the restitution of our rights. Defended and sheltered by them, we feel stronger and entitled to collect from those who would damage or steal our belongings and rob us of our liberties.

Teachers

Teachers educate us to be members of society. By passing down the collective wisdom, teachers create a productive citizenry that contributes to the maintenance and momentum of society. Our national security depends on a well-educated population to maintain our esteemed place in the world. At the highest level, teachers preserve our nation by tapping into, actualizing, and channeling the creative energy in each of us. They feed our hungry minds. Whether we thirst for mastery or for the opportunity to discover, we are drawn like magnets to new information and new ideas. Working inside the mind to unleash our potential, educators can broaden our worldview and expand the horizons of the possible.

Clerics

Clerics guide us toward developing a moral code for living. Called to belong, to be part of a higher spiritual community, we are sustained by the unity and wholeness of a larger fellowship. Although some of us believe God may bring us into being, how we live day to day endows our lives with substance and meaning. Clerics remind us that we can go beyond ourselves. They address our aloneness and our apprehension about our mortality. They direct our eyes and open doors to the mysteries of the unknown. Indeed, when we transcend our limitations, we give our lives a fuller purpose that reduces our isolation. Given moral direction for living by clerics, we are invited to trust and believe in that which we cannot see so that we can allay our fear of letting go and our apprehension about the hereafter. We then can use our energies for solving complex personal and social problems and making the world a better place to live.

Psychotherapists

The most recent arrivals to the family of professionals, psychotherapists attend to our psychic pain. Psychotherapy has evolved in response to the needs of people whose suffering reflects a psychologically unhealthy society. Living with low self-esteem, people in pain forfeit who they are to the definitions of others and buy society's materialistic advertisement for the "good and successful life." Acting as an antidote to a depersonalized, accelerated, and consuming society, many therapists seek to hold out the possibility of an alternative set of values; they form a countermovement that instead fosters an internalized sense of worth and self-definition. They teach the process of relationships and provide the caring that nurtures healing and growth. These secular clerics treat the fallout from society's ills and problems. Ideally, they unburden us of the millstones of helplessness, hopelessness, anxiety, and depression that cripple our spirits and injure our connections with others.

SOCIETY'S ROLE

For the most part, as members of society, we both set professionals apart and elevate them into privileged positions of power. "I saw him as someone who could be strong for me when I could not be strong for myself, a champion, a guiding light, a conqueror of ills," said a client. Whether our hero or heroine is called doctor, counselor, professor, or pastor, we simultaneously acknowledge the difference in status and honor the professional by using his or her title.

Unlike the shaman, whose powers derive from spirits and whose reputation is established by feats of supernatural consequence, professionals' competence is temporally based and their power derives primarily from social attribution. The secular anointment we give is merely functional, in that it grants each type of professional the authority to enter the vulnerable places of our being for a specific purpose. We raise professionals high in esteem. Our deference to their seniority and our compliance with their directives establish our status as recipients. Such deference and compliance are essential to professionals' effectiveness.

Professional Privilege

We grant professionals who enter our lives major license to direct and even determine the flow of events that comprise our existence. In both subtle and overt ways, they influence and manage our choices. We empower and reward them for their services by bestowing a host of advantages that demarcate their special and privileged status and further bolster their authority.

Professional Discretion and Control of Choice

While Western society rests on freedom of choice for its individual members, it also grants professionals a significant degree of autonomy to make decisions that significantly affect each of our realities. The phrase "professional discretion," for example, entitles professionals to exercise independent judgment that is monitored in only limited ways by others.

The therapist decides how dangerous a case of abuse is and whether to report it to child protection services. The lawyer determines whether our case is substantial enough to warrant legal representation. The cleric can elect not to perform a marriage if our chosen partner is not of the appropriate religious persuasion. The academic advisor judges the thoroughness of our research and approves or delays our degree. The physician evaluates whether our physical injury is serious enough to justify Social Security assistance. Certainly, we retain some measure of autonomy and choice about our situations. We can decide what we will do about our abusive behavior. We can take alternative routes to settle disputes or interview other lawyers about the efficacy of our case. We can search out a cleric willing to officiate at our life-cycle events. We can appeal the decision of an academic advisor or transfer to another institution. We can find a physician who is apt to understand our limitations when evaluating our condition for Social Security benefits. We can also explore alternative income-producing possibilities.

Yet, juxtaposed against our ability to be self-determining is professional power. "The magnitude of the power is absolutely incredible," acknowledged an attorney. "The judge decides who puts money in an envelope instead of coming to court for a traffic ticket, who wins and loses in lawsuits, who gets the kids, who goes to jail or is placed on probation, and whose case will or will not be dismissed. These are decisions about reward and punishment. In a sense, these verdicts establish who gets the privilege."

A physician described how the economic decisions he made could affect a patient's care. "As a heart surgeon, I see a patient and prescribe nitroglycerin. I make $3 on the office visit. But if I carry him through the heart operation, there's $10,000 in my pocket. Or perhaps I jointly own equipment with other physicians in the community. Every time I order a test that requires use of that equipment, there's a dime in my pocket. These are crude examples, but we make these determinations all the time."

A psychologist remarked, "In my work, I make all kinds of treatment decisions. While I hope my recommendations are built on solid clinical evidence, my personal reactions to clients certainly sway me. I decide who is referred for chemical dependency evaluation, who is sent to the hospital, who may need antidepressants, and who is placed in foster care. Nowadays even the diagnosis I make allows some clients to obtain extended insurance benefits, while others receive only Band-Aid treatment."

Professional Discretion and Control of Time

In addition to controlling important aspects of our lives, professionals govern the time they spend with us. By controlling our time together, they control the interaction between us. They structure when, to whom, and for how long we can talk. We unconsciously relinquish our managing of time to have access to what we need from them. Although professionals never declare their prerogative, we gradually learn "how it is" through experience.

In the classroom, teachers govern discussion. They decide whether the class will be lecture or seminar, experiential or didactic. They decide which students to favor and which to dismiss. They determine whether students can express their opinions or disagree. They decide whether they will or will not tolerate "wrong-minded" interpretations. They dictate how much of a student's idea they will let the rest of the class hear.

In the lawyer's office, "billable hours" means that talking costs so much per minute. In the courtroom, the lawyer commands that we silence our own voice while he or she speaks on our behalf. Lengthy depositions become contests of time, tournaments of endurance and will. We are commanded to respond precisely to the opposing attorney's meticulously worded questions, inferences, and accusations.

The therapeutic session is carefully orchestrated by the clock and by the therapist's response to our concerns. Like conductors of symphony orchestras, therapists cue us about what they want to hear and when they want to hear it. They ask leading questions and monitor how long we spend talking about particular issues. They decide whether the session will focus on our current feelings or our early childhood experiences. They make the rules about whether we can argue or are merely expected to listen. They set the limit for how much of ourselves we can show.

The religious service is a forum for the cleric's message. As members of the congregation, we listen to the cleric's selection of lessons and commandments without interruption. Whether bored or enthralled, we respect the cleric's sovereignty and stay in our seats. Outside the service, the cleric directs the timing of events. In some denominations, clerics structure the confessional and control the substance and length of our penance. We obey clerics who tell us when to light candles, how long to fast, when and in what language to say prayers.

Waiting for the physician is a culturally recognized admission of privilege. The 15-minute office visit limits how many questions we can ask and how much information we receive. Some procedures, such as Pap smears, require advance patient preparation; without such adequate groundwork, a 10-minute procedure can feel psychologically and physically intrusive. Knowing the doctor is busy and behind schedule structures our response. We feel grateful. We keep our requests to a minimum or hesitate to ask an anxious question. One doctor wrote, "Practically any interchange could be cut short on the basis of my busyness. All I had to do was stand up and patients knew they had only a little time left." Some training institutions even teach medical students "leave-taking" behaviors to help them extricate themselves from patients.

Social Dispensation and Reward

Having given professionals the right to exercise their authority in our lives, society compensates them for their service to us through social recognition and privilege. Professionals are allowed to play by a different set of rules, thus sparing them from the usual and mundane. This form of payment sanctions and honors their contribution while further strengthening their authority in our eyes. For example, the granting of tenure to senior clerics, judges, and full professors allows them to enjoy a stable career for a lifetime. A university administrator explained, "Tenure is a privilege we give practically no one else in this society. It is an incredible power without accountability. It means that unless you shoot your mother on the street, we're not going to fire you. In fact, if someone does a very poor job, the university doesn't break tenure anymore. Instead, you are bought out. Professors may act as outrageously as possible to land a big settlement."

While not all professionals enjoy a guaranteed job, many of them are paid handsomely for their efforts, which further establishes their rank as members of an elite class. In some instances, professionals receive special financial dispensations and preferential treatment. "Ministers in our region get discounts on cars," explained a cleric. "It happens all the time, and some clergy brag about it. I get a 20% discount on my allergy bill. Some of my colleagues get free country club memberships. Somehow you have this grace-filled life and you don't have to earn it the way everybody else does." "Professional courtesy" accords physicians' families free medical treatment from other physicians. Professionals who attend conferences in other countries can claim travel as an educational expense. While these and other perks produce some financial advantage, their real value is the accrual of social recognition and entitlement that accompany each benefit.

Some of this recognition is conferred through special tributes or symbols of achievement. Holding offices in professional societies, being selected for civic and cultural boards, and being awarded sabbaticals, research grants, or fellowships all create a lofty and desirable image. These public and prestigious awards further legitimize the professional's power and instill within us a deep regard for his or her talents and accomplishments. As an attorney remarked, "Being a professional is something you strive for. People have a lack of respect for the ordinary man, but if you're a professional, it's different. People's whole attitudes shift when they find out. Even if they think you're goofy, they are apprehensive and their manner changes."

Cooperation and Compliance

Acceptance of professional privilege and professionals' prerogatives permeates our society. We are conditioned as children to accept professionals' power and superiority as normal. We participate by acquiescing to their directives. Being a "good" student or patient, for example, implies that our cooperation makes the professional's job easier. Our deference toward professionals and their authority is bolstered by societal prescription and reinforced by the media and the pressure to conform. Everybody does it like we do. While we may not willingly participate in the rituals of the classroom, law office, medical examination room, religious service, or therapy session, we nonetheless conform to solve a problem or accomplish a goal. Our compliance symbolically reaffirms our high regard for the professional's role and the person who occupies the position. It links us to the professional and elevates the professional in our mind. In fact, we are the "society" that sanctions their privilege by virtue of our deference to their authority.

Childhood Preparation

Since earliest childhood, we are taught to respect, admire, and obey the professional. Our mothers and fathers willingly allow the physician to touch and examine our bodies. Against our most vocal protests, we receive shots and swallow foul-tasting medicines. Clergy are an integral part of our early life-cycle events: Our parents have them officiate at our circumcision or baptism, our first communion, our confirmation, or bar or bat mitzvah. Typically, teachers represent our first sustained contact with adults other than our parents and immediate relatives. They tell us what to do and when to do it, they monitor our relationships with other children, and they praise or criticize our performance. The teacher, doctor, or minister dictates what is good, what is right. As children, we observe our parents' deferential attitudes toward professional authority and follow their teachings. We trust our parents' beliefs and transfer that trust to all professionals.

Conditioned Responses

In addition to childhood conditioning, repetitive social conditioning reinforces our deference. We rise when the judge enters the courtroom, we wait for the doctor, we follow the script and consult our attorney first, we raise our hands in class to ask for the teacher's permission to speak, and we divulge to the therapist the most intimate aspects of our lives. Our behavior reminds us that professionals know more, they are in charge, and they will establish the rules. We are to listen attentively, show them proper respect, and comply with their instructions. Until there is substantial reason to doubt the professional's credibility, we accept the difference in status as a societal norm.

Professionals themselves are surprised by the manifestations of our social conditioning. They do not recognize their images in the mirror of our response. "As a medical student with a very limited base of knowledge," said one physician, "I would walk onto a ward and people would be in awe. I could say to a patient, 'Gee, your socks are on backward.' And he or she would say, 'Thank you for that god-inspired message.' That doesn't happen to my other friends in other walks of life." A therapist said, "The whole time my child was in school, his teachers would tell me he was lucky to have a psychologist for a mother. They believed that since I had knowledge about human behavior, I automatically could turn out wonderful children." "I can get on the phone and make a lot of strange things happen," added a judge. "If I make the reservation for dinner tonight, we'll get in probably whenever we want. It's downright embarrassing. You'd think we were borne in by vapors. The sea parts and we walk on dry land. It's really rather funny, but it's also very uncomfortable. You come to believe you're special in some very important ways."

While we are products of our childhood and social conditioning, our cooperation and compliance change with age and change again because of our experiences. Many of us, for example, have vivid memories of professionals and how they treated us as children; some of us carry the relationships inside and use them as models in our adult relationships with professionals. As we grow older, however, most of us become more prudent and less idealistic. We take back some of the godlike status we gave to professionals when we were children. Our expectations become more realistic and we are more accepting of who they are as people. There is more room for a give-and-take between us. The maturity of these responses, however, often disintegrates during times of crisis. When we are in a position of extreme need, helplessness, or dependency, we revert to childlike postures based on the degree of trauma we experience. At these moments, we believe that our cooperation and compliance with the professional's directives are essential for a positive outcome. The general social regard paid professionals becomes the insurance policy that guarantees their attention during these vulnerable periods in our lives.

THE ETHOS OF CARE

From the client's perspective, professionals' authority and compliance with it are the means to achieving a common purpose. While the arrangement between professional and client can be viewed as a secular contract, this perspective is too simplistic and reductionistic. Such a view cancels out the essential, though less visible, element of faith. Yet, it is our faith in the professional's abilities to respond to our needs that enables us to comply automatically and without hesitation.

Before we confer our faith, however, we have to believe that professionals will place our needs before their own. This inherent ethos of care has the force of a profound and, in effect, sacred moral authority. For us to follow their lead into unknown territory assumes and therefore requires a depth of care and commitment from professionals that raises the relationship to a sacred covenant of fidelity and obligation. Rooted in biblical and spiritual tradition, the covenant between us is currently expressed through professional codes and statements of purpose.

The Covenant

Law, therapy, medicine, teaching, and religion are professions that enshrine a meaningfulness to their calling, an avowal to a higher purpose.

Professionals who enter these fields implicitly take a solemn vow of personal dedication to their social responsibility. They are granted the rights of power over other people's lives. In return for this privilege, they promise to abide by and keep sacrosanct certain practices and ideals.

The depth of meaning associated with this exchange is expressed through the covenant, a contract common to all civilizations. In Western theology, it is popularly referenced in the story of Abraham, who is considered the progenitor of the Jewish people. God makes a covenant with Abraham: He will make Abraham, at age 99, exceedingly fruitful, thus establishing his progeny as the chosen people. In exchange, Abraham promises to serve God and abide by his law. He proves his faith by agreeing that every manchild shall be circumcised as a token of the covenant. Abraham twice obligates himself—to his people and to his God.

Like Abraham, professionals profess a dual affiliation. Indeed, the binding quality of their covenant with us grows out of their dual obligation to (1) take care of the person being represented, treated, taught, or ministered to and (2) work within the context of hallowed and transcendent principles. Operating within this dual framework keeps professionals ethically grounded and centrally focused on our needs.

Codes of Ethics, Statements of Purpose

Just as professionals are today's secular shamans, the oaths and codes of each profession are the secular expressions of the sacred covenant. In the past, society joined the sacred and secular realms. Today's society treats these two arenas as unrelated kin. Because the concept of letting go and having faith in professionals rests on a spiritual base, however, the metaphysical dimension within the social contract has not vanished. Through professional codes, professionals try to retain the spiritual base of our agreement but in disguised and diluted form.

The Hippocratic oath defines, in covenant terms, the obligations of a physician. This intrinsically religious promise directs the physician's voice to the gods from whose power the profession of healing derives and who decree his or her duties to patients. "I swear by Apollo Physician, and Asclepius and Hygieia, and Panaceia that I will fulfill according to my ability and judgment this oath and this covenant. . . . In purity and holiness I will guard my life and my art. . . . If I fulfill this oath and do not violate it, may it be granted to me to enjoy life and art . . . ; if I transgress it and swear falsely, may the opposite of all this be my lot" (Edelstein, 1967, p. 6).

Within the field of law, attorneys vow to uphold the Model Code of Professional Responsibility (American Bar Association, 1990). Instead of swearing by the gods, attorneys declare an allegiance to justice and the dignity of the individual. "[A] free and democratic society . . . is based upon . . . law grounded in respect for the individual and his capacity through reason for enlightened self-government. Law so grounded makes justice possible. . . . Lawyers, as guardians of the law, play a vital role in the preservation of society. . . . Within the framework of these principles, a lawyer must with courage and foresight be able and ready to shape the body of law to the ever-changing relationships of society. . . . So long as its practitioners are guided by these principles, the law will continue to be a noble profession. This is its greatness and its strength, which permit of no compromise" (Preamble).

Each religious denomination has its own ordination rites. Initiates declare their beliefs that bind them to God and to their obligations to the community. In the Episcopal church (Book of Common Prayer, 1979), the bishop charges, "My brother [or sister], the Church is the family of God, the body of Christ, and the temple of the Holy Spirit. . . . As a priest, it will be your task to proclaim by word and deed the Gospel of Jesus Christ, and to fashion your life in accordance with its precepts. You are to love and serve the people among whom you work, caring alike for young and old, strong and weak, rich and poor. . . . In all that you do, you are to nourish Christ's people from the riches of his grace, and strengthen them to glorify God in this life and in the life to come. . . . My brother [or sister], do you believe that you are truly called by God and his church to the priesthood? ['I believe I am so called.'] Do you now in the presence of the Church commit yourself to this trust and responsibility? ['I do.']" (p. 531).

Like other professionals, therapists are mandated to follow the code of ethics of their respective disciplines. The Preamble to the Code of Ethics for Clinical Social Workers (1988) states, "Ethical principles affecting the practice of clinical social work are rooted in the basic values of society and the social work profession. The principal objective of the profession of clinical social work is to enhance the dignity and well-being of each individual. . . . The primary goal of this code . . . is to offer general principles [to social workers] to guide their conduct and to inspire their will to act according to ethical principles in all of their professional functions" (p. 9).

While the profession of teaching, as understood by the circles in higher education, requires no explicit oath, there is an implied obligation to students by virtue of working for an institution whose purpose is education. For example, one liberal arts college (Macalester College, 1988) declares in its Statement of Purpose and Belief that "it is dedicated to the intellectual and personal growth of its members, it cherishes and strives to nurture each individual's capacities for compassion, understanding, judgment, knowledge and action. . . . We believe that teaching and learning are the central activities of this institution. This means that in the composite of teaching, service and research generally expected of faculties, the primary responsibility is teaching which fosters the intellectual growth of the students" (p. 6).

THE PROFESSIONAL-CLIENT RELATIONSHIP

The covenant of understanding exemplified in the professional codes establishes the base of the connection between us and professionals. It forms the essential affiliation and breathes life into the process of the relationship. Whether the professional is a physician, cleric, teacher, therapist, or attorney, everything he or she does flows through the medium of relationship. Whether or not professionals are aware of it, we as clients carry the connection inside us. "I forget how singular a doctor is in people's lives," said a female physician. "I'm their doctor, but they are not my only patient. One poor fellow was at a gathering and we were being introduced. He said, 'Oh, you're my physician. You just gave me a physical exam.' He turned scarlet. I had no recollection. 'Don't worry,' I said. 'I don't remember people when they have their clothes on.' I'm sure he was vividly remembering everything that I had done and expected me to see the same picture. I didn't recognize him at all."

Regardless of whether the professional establishes a personal connection with each patient, each student, or each parishioner, our trust as clients cannot be given in a relational vacuum. Whether built on a few cursory words, a visual picture, or the legacy of a reputation, we sustain the connection with imagery and through it allow ourselves to be touched, inspired, and persuaded.

Our Trust

While the professional-client relationship is built on the professional's expert authority and his or her obligation to serve, our surrender of the particular aspects of our "soul" that need special care is central to the intent of the association. The concept of "turning over" requires us as clients to relinquish control. However, because control is every human being's form of self-protection, handing it over leaves us vulnerable. When we allow ourselves to enter into the process of care with the professional, we let go of managing the outcome.

As clients, we believe that our job is to trust. One client, in writing her story, described her struggle to trust a therapist who was abusing her. She thought that her journey depended on her ability to believe in him.

She mistakenly believed that her distrust of him reflected her deficiencies as a patient.

"You fantasize about me, don't you?" he asked. Tears began to flow. "Yes," I lied, but the tears continued. Why wasn't I having fantasies? What was wrong with me? Wouldn't it be wonderful to fantasize about this brilliant therapist, someone everyone looked up to? I should be honored that he cared about me. If I could just identify more closely with him through my fantasies, he could help me past my sense of injury. So I must trust him, trust him more.

This client believed that she had to trust in order to get better. She transferred this expectation onto the therapist and believed that she could not learn to trust if she did not trust him. Such an act of giving over, of trusting, highlights the spiritual nature of the relationship. As we surrender voluntarily or involuntarily those parts of ourselves that need tending, we become vulnerable. We use our trust to assuage how defenseless we feel. We fill in the void with our faith.

Professionals' Restraint

Our trust rests on the assumption that professionals will operate within the context of our needs. This precept requires of professionals a constant vigilance to what is best for us. "The understanding that the client's needs will come before mine is an act of moderation," declared an attorney. "I may have wonderful ideas that I think will transform this person's life, but I have to keep asking, 'Is this for me or is this really best for the other person?' Being a professional means not just exercising a skill; rather, there is a responsibility to the person with whom I am dealing." Being responsible to clients means that professionals agree to monitor their self-interests while operating within the context of the relationship. Professionals, too, have to enter the process of care and shape what they have to offer to fit the individual client.

Endemic to the concept of professionalism is self-restraint. If professionals do not channel and discipline themselves, we as clients lose. In contrast to business, where the profit motive is king, professionals make a covenant with the larger society and with each client to give, not take. This constant challenge follows professionals like a shadow.

Professionals themselves are exquisitely conscious of the temptations to reorder their priorities and abandon their primary commitment to clients' needs. "Let's say I'm a research-oriented person," said one physician. "It furthers my career to carry out a research project over a period of years. I can get patients to consent anytime depending on how I present the idea. In some institutions, 95% of the patients participate in various studies. When I offer my patients similar alternatives, they bend away from research. Only 5 to 10% go on a study. That's a striking difference. I don't believe that the patients differ, but the physicians differ in how they present their positions."

A therapist gave another example: "I live in a small community and see clients who know the same people I know. One of my clients is on the city council and knows lots of people. When he talked about his next-door neighbors, I could tell from his description that they go to my church. I'd even been to a dinner party with them. Then he talked about some other folks who lived in the next town. He described a teacher married to an accountant. Everyone he mentioned, I knew. I almost got into the 'Oh, that must be so-and-so game' with myself. They were all interesting people, and it was tempting to learn more about their lives. What an opportunity for me to get information and to ask questions to satisfy my own interests rather than to take care of what my client needed! Living in a small town, I have to monitor myself constantly not to be just curious."

Such nonindulgence is richly rewarded. In exchange for this ascetic practice, the professional gains our respect. Wealth is measured by reputation, not by dollars. "It's a trade-off," said a cleric. "In exchange for being responsible for others, showing restraint, making a commitment, and accepting a fiduciary position, you gain respectability. It allows you to feel worthy, to be part of something larger that protects the society. You don't need any more than that. It's an immediate ascendancy."

RISKS TO THE HEALTH OF THE RELATIONSHIP

The professional-client relationship can be—and usually is—viewed through a purely secular lens. We are comfortable with this functional explanation of our relationship because it is rational and logical. The less visible and irrational aspects of our faith and trust complicate this otherwise simple and tidy arrangement. So does the element of the professional's caring, which is voluntary and cannot be elicited on demand. By secularizing each profession, society has camouflaged the spiritual essence and base of the connection. From this vantage point, it is tempting to redefine the relationship as a business venture that is commercially motivated rather than as a partnership of trust and professional self-restraint. Keeping the more spiritual aspects hidden is dangerous. Making them covert allows professionals to deny the emotional significance of the relationship. Minimizing the importance of the connection weakens the covenant and opens the way for boundary violations.

Operating outside the boundaries of self-restraint, some professionals at times place their own needs first and violate the reason for the relationship. "I came to you because of my need," said one client to a professional. "I gave you my trust. You failed to exercise restraint. Because of that, there is pain between us." When professionals indulge themselves, their primary relationship is not with our needs but rather with themselves and their own best interests. They ignore the primacy of the covenant. This lack of allegiance to their own professional values and to us as clients undoes the pact between us. Our trust is violated. The core of our connection is broken.

Because the spiritual values that form the base of the connection are hidden or minimized, professionals and clients alike may not be aware of violations. Thus, a violation can stay underground. All too often our suffering remains locked inside us. Unsure of our rights, worried about our needs, and not wanting to jeopardize our future, we often silence our voices and mask our injuries. Even though we make ourselves mute in front of others, our internal conversations are loud. We silently scream at the doctor who keeps us waiting in the "waiting" room. We feel humiliated by the pastor who referred to our personal situation in his Sunday sermon. We are outraged at the attorney who "forgot" to file the necessary papers in court. We feel anxious and apprehensive around the professor who looks at us whenever he tells a sexually suggestive joke. We are confused by and uncomfortable with the therapist who tells us about her personal history and problems.

While many of our contacts with professionals are completely satisfactory, there are too many instances where the contact is otherwise. Generally, we do not express what we really think and feel. Because of the professional's power and our compliance, we do not have access to our voices. Indeed, we forget that we need ultimately to be responsible for ourselves. Believing we have no choice, we adjust ourselves and endure the professional's inappropriate behavior. We blame ourselves, minimize our pain, and bury our reactions.

Why do we as clients go along with inappropriate behavior from professionals? What keeps us quiet and subservient in their presence? Why do we abide situations that offend us? What allows us to dismiss reprehensible circumstances, thereby normalizing conduct we otherwise deplore? The answer is simple. We worry that challenging the professional's inappropriate behavior could negatively affect his or her attitudes toward us and his or her concern for our welfare. The threat of abandonment and terror of the unknown reawaken our primal fears. We know we need what professionals have to offer. Even if we are cynical, we know the good that professionals can do for us and we want to count on their help. Even when professionals disappoint us, we often continue to hope that our next encounters will be different. Since we are partially dependent creatures and cannot fully care for ourselves, we prefer to pay the cost of tolerating painful experiences rather than ending up alone.

II

THE POWER DIFFERENTIAL IN THE PROFESSIONAL-CLIENT RELATIONSHIP

A S CLIENTS, WE ARE VULNERABLE because of needs that we cannot take care of ourselves. Professionals, because of their training and expertise, are better equipped to meet these needs. The potential for boundary violations derives from the space that exists between the knowledgeable professional and the vulnerable client. The inequality between us, the power differential, creates the need for protection. Boundaries define formally and informally how professionals are to exercise their power inside the relationship. When professionals maintain these limits, the power differential presents no problems. However, when professionals abuse the privilege of their power, they violate the boundary that protects the space and place us in jeopardy.

SOURCES OF CLIENTS' VULNERABILITY

As clients, we are vulnerable fourfold: (1) to the dictates of our needs, (2) to our need for resolution, (3) to our inability to take care of our needs alone, and (4) to professionals' influence in our lives. Our needs demand our attention and order the priorities in our lives. Like hungry children, we cannot fully proceed with our broader individual agendas until we first address our immediate nutritional concerns. The process of living continuously creates new challenges, persistently confronting us with our fundamental dependency on others for what we do not have or cannot do. Since many of these challenges can only be addressed by professionals, their influence in our lives is substantial and etched deeply into our memories.

Our needs and the conditions that produce them are an ongoing flow of events that span the map of possibilities. As a client said, "Like the surf in the ocean, life just keeps coming at you." Whether we need the assistance of a lawyer to set up guardianship for our children in the event of our death, the wisdom of a rabbi about how to approach an estranged relative, the attention of a teacher to foster our talents in a personally meaningful direction, the commitment of a physician to steer us through a serious illness, or the steadfast understanding of a therapist to help us unravel the secret of sexual abuse in our family, we cannot move on with life until our specific need is met. Our longing for resolution not only leads us ultimately to rely on the skills of professionals but also increases our sense of need in the meantime. Indeed, having to wait for answers often heightens our anxiety and intensifies how vulnerable we feel.

Our hunger grows as we recognize our own human limits and inability to satisfy our needs by ourselves. We alone cannot educate ourselves fully enough to survive. We do not have the knowledge to prescribe the correct medication for our medical condition. We cannot officiate at our own wedding or represent ourselves in a court of law.

Being dependent on professionals for what we cannot do for ourselves exposes our need to others, making us feel even more vulnerable. In addition, we have to forego the time we customarily spend building trust with strangers. When those "strangers" come from a different culture or are of a different gender, race, sexual orientation, educational level, or socioeconomic class, the differences between us multiply, so that we are additionally vulnerable to how social attitudes can affect the responses of professionals to our needs.

We mitigate the terror of our vulnerability by allowing ourselves to be dependent and, therefore, less alone. An attorney observed, "Many people are dissatisfied with their lawyer, but they keep going because they are afraid of what the alternative might be. They have so much energy and money invested that even though they don't like this person, they stick with him or her until the bitter end." We repress the magnitude and depth of our dependency, however, until we are faced with the possibility of losing whom or what we need. As a client said in describing her initial reaction to her therapist's absence at a critical time in her life, "I felt so powerless that I almost passed out, like everything I had gained was being taken away."

SOURCES OF PROFESSIONAL POWER

The obligation of professionals is to use their power to meet our needs and make a positive difference in our lives. Though invisible and elusive, the potency of their power is obvious when patients get better, legal clients gain a sense of justice from a jury's verdict, or the laity feel uplifted after a service. This power derives from four sources that, collectively, establish professionals' authority.

Societal Ascription

Society both charges and grants professionals the right to use their power for the benefit of others. Their actions are made credible because their role is sanctioned and protected by law and buttressed by social institutions. Physicians cannot practice without a license. Teachers cannot teach without proper credentials. Lawyers cannot represent clients without being admitted to the state bar.

Because we are conditioned to accept the social structure and values that legitimize professionals' power, we accept their authority as part of a normative process. We voluntarily comply. Because of social conditioning and professional training, professionals learn to exercise the authority prescribed by their role. They expect their directives to be accepted. We endorse their authority by cooperating.

Expert Knowledge

The professional's knowledge is a storehouse of resources desired by clients. Knowing what to do and knowing what will work form the basis of the professional's competence. Since information is used to influence and convince, this powerful commodity has the potential to change lives. Robert Veatch (1985) has pointed out that the Hippocratic oath was framed around the belief that "[k]nowledge was considered to be too esoteric—too dangerous and too powerful to be revealed to outsiders. This is why the Hippocratic Oath contains a pledge of secrecy. The oath was created by a group in the same way that a religious cult would create a code for its members" (p. 209).

This same thought is echoed by an attorney: "Professionals hold the keys. They control the amount of information and explanation given to the client. But the client has access only to the system or the device that enables a client to achieve what he or she wants through the professional's explanation or translation. After all, if everybody knows what I know and everybody can talk about it, what good am I?"

Since professionals' knowledge and expertise light the way for clients, most of us view these holders of such specialized information as wise and masterly. Referring to a physician, a client said, "My daughter had brain surgery. There's something incredible about somebody who spends six hours in surgery and solves this problem. Giving the gift of life is a pretty big deal." Not surprisingly, we clients often regard the mastery of professionals as complex and esoteric. This belief imbues the professional's competence with mystery. "At a cocktail party, everyone thinks you can read their mind," said a therapist. "It's like you have a crystal ball and know their private histories just from how they behave with you."

Because professionals possess such specialized knowledge and skill, we clients separate ourselves as commoners from professionals as experts. Because of their training, professionals control the resources we need. They know how the system works. In contrast, we do not have the tools to evaluate the merits of their advice and therefore may have to make decisions based on their ascribed rather than their demonstrated competence. Once a particular professional's superior competence is established, we give considerable weight to his or her thoughts and direction and accept as valid his or her definition of our reality.

Clients' Expectations and Projections

As clients, we all need a personal connection with those who touch the significant and sometimes intimate aspects of our lives. We must become acquainted with these strangers. Sometimes we come to know them well. Other times we fill the relational voids with images created out of bits and pieces of information. We draw upon these images and use our memories to create or recall the inner experience of a personal connection. We attach ourselves in order to be touched. We bond to trust. The energy generated by this silent coupling infuses professionals with power.

We give power to professionals out of our neediness. The more distressed we are, the more powerful professionals become. Professionals are the recipients of our secret hopes, anxieties, and defenses. In fact, we project parts of ourselves onto professionals and, through them, act out our inner debates. With physicians, we project our fears about the fragility of life and the awesome regard for its wonder. With lawyers, we project our conflicts about good and bad, right and wrongdoing, justice and injustice. With clerics, we project our questions of conscience and approach them as judges or givers of mercy and comfort. With therapists, we project our shame about our dark side and our longing for acceptance. With teachers, we project our hopes about whom and what we can become.

We also relate to professionals out of our childhood experiences with authority figures. If we were abused in our family, we may be careful not to question the professional. If we were neglected, we may hunger after a warm and sympathetic ear. If we fought our parents for control, we may respond combatively and battle the professional for the power. If the professional does not understand the origin of our presumptive response, has no limits, or is frightened of our anger, he or she may inadvertently feed our paranoia or encourage the negative ways we express our entitlement.

Other expectations derive from the ideal images stored in the our psyches. Frequently, professionals are unknowingly measured by us against these images. When the reality matches the model, the professional is accorded even greater esteem. If a student holds a professor in high regard, the student sees him or her as wise and astute, learned and all-knowing. If a physician helps a patient feel better, he or she becomes a tower of strength with godlike dimensions. All of the morally and ethically based professions have a fiduciary component that calls the professional to hold part of the client's well-being in trust. This reality (which elevates the professional), plus the client's neediness, stimulates these expectations and reawakens dormant childlike postures of dependency.

Our expectations and our hopes, as well as our projections onto the professional, are a covert source of power. Sometimes this projective process is called transference. Other times it is called dependency. It operates in all relationships to some degree but is much more evident with authority figures than with peers.

This invisible power is frequently misunderstood. Professionals who have little direct client involvement find it particularly difficult to comprehend the magnitude of the power given by a client's expectations and projections. Unable to incorporate this reality, professionals other than therapists tend to regard natural dependency issues as inappropriate, immature, or distorted. They dismiss them as foreign and inconsequential to the business at hand.

Refusing to acknowledge the client's reality does not make it disappear, however. Even though professionals — except for therapists — mentally banish the actuality of the power that derives from their clients' emotional truth, its existence is pervasive and strongly influences the reality of professionals' authority in clients' lives. A patient described how strongly she wanted the approval of a physician who specialized in working with overweight women. Following her weight loss, she discussed the possibility of surgery to enlarge her breasts: "My physician told me they looked fine to him. Since he approved of them, I felt wonderful. I will always remember that. I got the high that I was looking for."

A client described her reaction to the attorney who rescued her life savings in a court battle: "I was alone and vulnerable. I had no money. He fit everything from father figure to protector. In the courtroom, I felt like I was watching my boyfriend beat up someone who had hurt me. In a very classy way, he tore apart the man who robbed me. Sitting there and watching that, I was absolutely bonded to him for life."

A student described how much he admired a teacher who had coached him in softball when he was 14 years old: "I just kept getting better and better. I felt real confident. It was a big ego boost. For the first time in my life, I was part of a team effort. I was in awe of him. I wanted to be liked by him. He had made everything all right. Because of his support, I couldn't do anything wrong. It was the most important time of my life." Since the student had been embarrassed by his limited athletic abilities, the teacher's singling him out to play first base significantly altered his self-perception and his behavior.

These stories provide the context for understanding the normal dimension of dependency in the professional-client relationship. Moreover, since our unstated expectations exponentially raise the amount of power we give professionals, professionals cannot afford an innocent or derisive posture around this component of their authority.

The Professional's Sense of Personal Power

Societal ascription, expert knowledge, and clients' unstated expectations are three sources of power that ultimately lie outside professionals. The fourth source exists within. "My power is core to me," said a psychologist. "It is who I am and how I know myself. It is my essence." Whether professional or client, how we express our power reflects our self-image. Our assertion of power is a statement of our individuality, a way of declaring our self-worth and value.

As with clients, how professionals handle their power is filtered through their childhood experiences with authority figures. They may replicate with their clients how they were treated as children. As one professional said, "When I was a child, my parents never imposed strict rules, but we all knew where the limits were. They engaged us in a Socratic dialogue so that we felt we were a part of the decision. I do the same thing now with my patients." Or they may do the opposite. They may fight against resembling their cowardly father or incompetent mother. They may feel repelled by the images of their dictatorial teachers or boring ministers. How they experience, structure, and react to their power is guided by these unconscious influences.

How they express their personal power is also guided by their feelings of self-worth and entitlement. If they feel powerless, they are uneasy about their rights; they do not feel legitimate. They wait for others to direct them. Concerned with safety, they take few risks. Sometimes they see themselves as victims. Other times they feel fraudulent and guilty. If, on the other hand, they feel omnipotent, they vest themselves with authority and feel special and unique. Self-righteously, they claim their jurisdictions as superior and self-important individuals. Needing to be right or seen as unassailable, they feed their grandiosity.

Either way, how professionals feel about themselves, how they feel about what they have to offer, and how they define themselves as authority figures diminish or augment their power. A physician shared a story that illustrated her introduction to her power and the risk she was to others.

> When I was a resident, a woman gave birth and then her uterus inverted. The doctor supervising me had me remove the placenta from the uterus, which was exactly the wrong thing to do. The patient began to bleed. We rushed her to the ER. It looked like we would have to do a hysterectomy. The anesthesiologist was an old general practice doc. He said, "Let me try it once." He was able to get the uterus back in.
>
> I was just blown away. I don't know how else to describe it. The patient nearly died and I was physically on the other end; I did the act. In retrospect, I don't think I caused it, but it's as close as I've ever been to killing somebody.
>
> That night I cried harder than at any other time I could remember. I wanted to be God. I didn't like the feeling of being able to make that kind of mistake. I didn't want it to happen again. I'm sure I could have decided, "I'm never going to get that close to another patient. I'm never going to do deliveries. I'm never going to do anything. I want to avoid this feeling." It was awful.
>
> There are times when we are making decisions quickly and there are big consequences. It's not like I'm God every day I make decisions, but the power is always there. Most situations aren't that vivid. It's more the subtle decisions we make. But that event was a watershed choice for me.

In this story, the patient gave over her physical welfare, and potentially her life, to the physician. The physician came face to face with the issue of her power. Knowing the patient could have died, she struggled against the reality of her power and the reality of her ignorance: "I wanted to be God. I didn't like the feeling of being able to make that kind of mistake." Precariously perched between these two realities, she felt her own and her patient's vulnerability to her mistakes. She considered escape: "I'm never going to get that close to another patient. I'm never going to do deliveries. I'm never going to do anything. I want to avoid this feeling."

How this physician worked through this incident influences how much at risk she and her future patients will be to her power. If she accepted her limitations, she might be more available emotionally, more tolerant of ambiguity, and more realistic about her competence. It would be easier for her to ask for help when she needed it. In contrast, if she insisted on being right, she might be less available to input from others, less tolerant of uncertainty, and more perfectionistic with herself and others. She might condemn herself for her mistakes or alternately hide them, even from herself. Struggling with judgments and issues of self-acceptance allows professionals to face and evolve their sense of personal power. Their experiences with themselves are fundamental to how they use their authority in their relationships with clients.

Professionals' power originates from these four sources—societal ascription, expert knowledge, clients' unstated expectations, and sense of personal power. It is an energy that professionals must harness to make change happen. Some of their power is connected to their role and function and some to external factors that influence each client's response. The remainder rests on their maturity and longevity in their respective fields.

THE POWER DIFFERENTIAL

The space between professionals' authority and clients' vulnerability creates a fundamental inequality in terms of who has the advantage in the relationship and the factors that diminish the client's ability to be self-determining. Moreover, as clients we add to our vulnerability by our decision to relinquish control to the professional, which throws into stark relief the power differential between us. By this act, we relinquish our power to be self-determining, which leaves us less self-protected.

Differences in Advantage

Being in need threatens our status as self-sufficient human beings. When we juxtapose ourselves against a knowledgeable and assured professional, we expose our lesser position. This basic fact establishes the professional's superior status.

Limits on Self-Determination

Turning over control – whether functionally or emotionally – to the professional creates the true vulnerability within the professional-client relationship. Of course, the setting and level of need vary from client to client. Clearly the vulnerability of a student in a classroom differs from that of a patient on an operating table, a client in a criminal proceeding, or a parishioner who seeks the advice of a cleric. In all instances, however, we temporarily relinquish some measure of our autonomy, which automatically restricts our ability to choose freely.

As clients, we are vulnerable for the following reasons:

• We are in one sense dependent consumers who are frequently uninformed as to what to expect from professionals. As petitioners, we must wait for their direction. Professionals, in contrast, know the territory well and use their influence to define reality for us.

• Our choices are limited, and the rational exercise of choice by each of us in this position is tempered by our concerns for how our choices could affect our safety in the relationship. The hallmark of professionals, however, is the capability of using a wide range of discretionary judgment in decision-making. Any hope that professionals will be accountable for their choices rests primarily on their voluntary self-monitoring.

• We do not know as much as professionals. Therefore, we lack the skills to evaluate their competence. Even after we are done using their services, we cannot always assess the adequacy of their performance. A client described how she had no base from which to measure the help she had received until she changed therapists and experienced the difference between them. "I really didn't know what therapy was all about. I was naive and just kept stumbling through things. Last February, I went to another therapist. The difference was day and night. In the five times I went to her, I learned more than in the four years I had spent with my previous therapist."

• We often do not have enough information to negotiate with professionals about our rights. Without their direction, we may not know the appropriate behaviors to assume. A nurse made some observations about the impact of current medical practice on patients' rights: "In school I learned that confidentiality was almost sacred. The public believes we practice that philosophy. Yet today if you show up in a hospital, you have several physicians, several nurses, someone interpreting lab work, a dozen technicians, a social worker, and the list goes on and on. The medical records are shared among the preapprovals, the insurance companies, the payers, and the whole health-care system. So the presumption about confidentiality is pretty shaky. But patients aren't aware of that fact."

• Our choices may be narrowed by the unavailability of professionals. In rural communities, for example, one church may serve all denominational needs. A college may have only one teacher who specializes in the subject matter you wish to pursue. Or a company plan or HMO may send someone only to a particular doctor. Whether grounded in reality or the result of a lack of knowledge, our belief that there are no alternatives gives us the sense of a monopoly, which further restricts our ability to choose.

• Our choices are restricted by time. When in the middle of a crisis, we have neither the time nor the motivation to shop around and dispassionately choose among alternatives. When we are confused or anxious, the influence of professionals often determines the direction we take.

• Our freedom to choose is affected by our anxieties about the future. Different from a reciprocal relationship in which the parties hold equal power, the asymmetric professional-client relationship makes it difficult for us as clients to feel free enough to disengage at will without risking our welfare. If a student drops a class because of the teacher's misconduct, for example, he or she might not be able to fulfill the requirements for his or her degree. More insidiously, we often do not feel free to disagree without having to worry about harmful consequences. Confronting a therapist, for example, could result in a punitive response.

THE FUNCTION OF BOUNDARIES

The power differential between professionals and clients impinges on the ability of clients to decide freely. Because professionals often shape our destiny, the limits on our self-determination leave us particularly vulnerable to their influence. Boundaries protect the space that must exist between professional and client by controlling the power differential in the relationship. They allow for a safe connection based on our needs, not those of the professional.

Boundaries regulate our interactions. "They define where I end and you start," said a therapist. "It's a way of saying what is mine, what I will allow and what I won't. They mark the territory between us." These demarcations provide us with a sense of personal privacy and safety. Operating within the boundaries that define a healthy professional-client relationship produces the consistency and predictability in behavior that lowers the risk to clients.

Rules and Regulations

Each profession has written policies and codes that enumerate the boundaries of professional conduct with clients. Principles of informed consent, confidentiality, the right to be served, equality of treatment, and fair and objective measures of student progress are but a few of these rules.

Each profession acknowledges the rights of clients by formalizing its obligations to clients within a code of conduct. In essence, codes are a form of boundary maintenance. They explicitly define the standards that are intended to safeguard the client's trust by restricting the professional's power. For example, rules about confidentiality attempt to guard the client's privacy by restricting the professional's freedom of disclosure. Rules about conflict of interest tend to guard the primacy of the client's need by restricting the professional's self-interest. Rules about competence and specialization presume to guard the quality of service to the client by restricting the professional's practice and sphere of expertise. Rules about termination seek to guard against potential client neglect and abandonment by restricting the conditions under which the professional can leave the relationship.

The general intent of these codes is to protect the client, who has less power in the relationship. Since codes are external to the process of the relationship, however, their protective ability is limited. While they intimate that our needs must come first, they give no practical working definition of what this means. While they try to establish the space between the professional and us as inviolable, the distance between the theory and the practice is extreme.

The Implicit Boundaries

Codes by themselves cannot possibly address all or even most of the situations encountered by professionals in the exercise of their authority. Moreover, their literal and narrow interpretation dangerously promotes the secularization of the spiritual dimension between professional and client.

In order to address our safety fully, professionals have to draw from a deeper well to determine the priorities and parameters between us and them. Indeed, within the spirit of the codes is the ethos of care, which guides our expectations of the relationship. The ethos of care has its own implicit boundaries, which prohibit actions that betray trust. The structure of the professional-client relationship derives from a relational model of care in which professionals are charged to (1) establish and maintain trust through their willingness to engage fully and respectfully with their clients; (2) take charge by accepting their authority and setting the tone and direction that keep the work focused and task oriented; (3) create and maintain a safe environment by establishing clear boundaries; and (4) define for us the behaviors that are necessary to fulfill our expectations by keeping us mindful of our power to effect our own decisions, aware of our responsibilities for ourselves, and cognizant of the need for feedback in the give-and-take that keeps the process between us healthy and current. Operating within a relational model imposes a natural constraint, in that it pulls professionals to remain sensitive to the power differential.

While these unspoken and less visible boundaries monitor the inequality between us, they also create the safety net of understanding that joins us in an agreed-upon and common purpose. This shared framework allows us as clients to comprehend what is happening to us and to presume the good intent and beneficial flow of the relationship. Such understanding is particularly evident in this physician's explanation to his patient about his behavior. "Sometimes I get angry," he said. "I'm not supposed to do that. I'm supposed to be a professional. But I'm just a human being in the real world and I have feelings too. When things are going well with you, I celebrate. By the same token, I also get blue and sad about a situation. I may have been angry the last time I saw you, but I don't remember that anymore. I'm your friend and I get angry with my friends and my children and my colleagues. Just because I raise my voice doesn't mean I care about you any less." While the appropriateness or inappropriateness of this physician's anger remains to be judged, he acknowledges the implicit boundaries mandated by the ethos of care when he expresses his concern about his impact on his patient.

When professionals operate within the explicit codes and implicit boundaries of the relationship, the power differential is contained. When they use their power outside these limits, the boundary that protects the space is violated. Since professionals govern significant parts of clients' lives, their use of authority is inherent in the professional-client relationship. Whether or not professionals actually acquiesce and accept this responsibility, the injunction to do so is clear.

As clients, we expect professionals to manage the boundary that maintains the natural asymmetry between us. This boundary exists for our protection. More fundamentally, it protects the relationship by keeping the space between us and professionals healthy and viable. Indeed, the professional's commitment to honor this boundary is part of the covenant that obliges professionals to act within the dictates of our needs. Our safety is compromised when the boundaries that guard our concerns are erased. The covenant that binds professionals to us is broken when they deny, ignore, or use the power differential in a way that negates the ethos of care.

III

THE PROFESSIONAL'S STRUGGLE WITH POWER

ALL OF US ARE CLIENTS DURING some parts of our lives. Only some of us are professionals too. In our role as professionals, we are at risk for causing or allowing boundary violations when we minimize our impact on clients by negating the magnitude of our power. Not being clear about who we are allows us to use the power differential to more easily shift the boundaries with our clients.

As professionals we clearly have more power than our clients. Yet, we generally do not feel all that powerful. We do feel responsible, however. While we are comfortable with the idea of being responsible, we do not always welcome the burdens it imposes. To redistribute the weight of our responsibility, we adopt a belief system that reduces the power differential in the relationship. We selectively blind ourselves to our impact when we use any of the following rationalizations or similar justifications: I'm just a vessel of the Lord. They're adults, they make their own decisions. We're all equal as human beings. Everyone can take care of himself or herself. For God's sake, I'm not going to inflate who I am. Well, they're consenting adults.

In addition to feeling burdened, professionals also feel tension. We are responsible for meeting the needs of others, but we cannot control the results longed for or expected by clients. Moreover, our effectiveness is dependent on our clients' cooperation and compliance. The paradox of being in charge while lacking control makes us feel unsure; we try to relieve this added pressure by being less in charge or more in control. While either move may reduce our discomfort, toying with the power differential again endangers our clients because the space between us is enlarged or minimized. Since our never being sure is an inherent part of the professional-client relationship, we professionals have to accept the difficult task of learning to live with the burdens and tensions of holding greater power in the relationship.

OUR AMBIVALENCE TOWARD POWER

As professionals, we make change happen. We use our power to make a difference. Whether we inspire a student to explore an innovative project, guide a patient through a chronic illness, or officiate and tend a family's grief at a funeral, we affect our clients' lives. While clients are well aware of our influence, we are usually more aware of the job to be done than of our power to accomplish it. Far from easily assimilating our power, most of us do not even realize the extent to which we have it.

Power itself is a constant; feeling powerful is mercurial. Since we only know our power through the difference we make in our clients' lives, the randomness and unpredictability of our impact lead us to experience power as an elusive energy that beckons, bombards, and hides. Since we can see our power only in the mirror of our clients' lives, this potent force is difficult to own. Although part of us and expressed through us, power is intangible and cannot be held or contained by us.

Even though we can name and describe the sources of professional power, we rarely identify ourselves as powerful. "I don't look upon myself as having a great deal of power," said a lawyer. "I may be troubled or frustrated by not being able to reach a goal, but I tend not to think about it in those terms." Our lack of acknowledgment occurs, in part, because some of our power originates from external sources. The power we derive from societal ascription and clients' unstated expectations feels outside of who we are. The power we derive from our sense of personal power may be only unconsciously exercised. Indeed, we tend to claim only the power we derive from our fund of expert knowledge. The rest of it seems separate from us and is, therefore, hard to accept.

"Power" is a hard word for professionals to use. It evokes images of oppression, competition, and being one-up. Questions about another's intentions follow close behind it. Such synonyms as "force," "control," "exploitation," "authority," "influence," and "dominance" arouse suspicion and produce volatile reactions. Surprised by such a response, others, in innocence or ernest denial, argue against these implications. Indeed, the potentially positive aspects of power are usually secondary, an after-thought, and emerge less potent than the negative aspects we fear.

Many of us are frightened of our power and how we might use it. A therapist observed, "Getting in touch with my power scared me because I realized what kind of impact I could have. I could be ruthless with my power. I got frightened because it didn't fit with who I thought I was. I didn't want to own my dark side. I would like to pretend I'm not that powerful. Yet, I know from being a parent, who felt overwhelmed and directionless, that everything I did shaped my child." Beginning profes-sionals particularly feel fraudulent because their lack of experience causes them to feel powerless and unworthy of the power ascribed by their role. A cleric expressed it this way: "When I saw the full size of my power, I wanted to run away and hide. No human being should have a right to have that kind of power over others. So when I saw it, I tried to backslide and backpedal."

Acknowledging our power means conceding the point that our clients have less than we do. Holding more power in the relationship can resurrect negative images of authority and oppression. Since we are in a caring position, these pictures run contrary to who we want to be to our clients. Furthermore, since we live in a democracy, we have difficulty integrating the discrepancy between our superior status and our treasured principles of equality. Finally, it is hard to admit that we gain pleasure and gratification as a result of having power over others.

RESPONSIBILITY AND TENSION

Even when we do not *feel* powerful, having more power creates the obligation to be aware of our impact on our clients. The burden imposed by this responsibility restricts our freedom, because we have to put the client first in the relationship. Keeping ourselves mindful of our greater power exposes the tension internal to us that inherently churns within the relationship. A teacher shared her struggle with having power and feeling responsible for how she used it:

It's very seductive to be given power. I am seduced by the role and I can seduce students with it. I know how to manipulate them into being responsive to what I teach. If I have a class that doesn't respond, I am so bummed out. Manipulation is positive when I use my students' minds to learn. But there's a fine line that can bleed into my students' feeding me. This is where my ego needs get met. The teaching dialogue is with myself. It's autoerotic. It's a high; it's like I've had a little shot of something. And my students feed my needs to be recognized and to be valued. There's a caste system in the class and everyone knows it. It's subtle. Whose names do I remember in the classroom? The ones who reflect back positively and the ones who reflect back negatively. I face a constant seduction to organize the class according to my needs.

Protection

Feeling responsible allows us to operate from a position of care and protects the primacy of our clients' needs. It serves to keep us humble in our mission and mindful of our impact. It functions as a check against our grandiosity. An oncologist shared how his concerns for the needs of his client helped him question the intent behind his decision: "I have lots of anxiety when I miss something or screw something up. There's so little that is black and white in medicine. I lay awake wondering about the decision I made at 11:30 at night. Did I make the decision because it was best for the patient or because it was the one that was least likely to get me up again at 3:00 in the morning?"

Decision-Making

Keeping ourselves observant, however, keeps us in a steady state of never being sure. We constantly have to make choices based on calculated risks. We have to assess where the need is, what to attend to, and which side to come down on this time. We try to make the right decision in part to relieve the tension. An attorney aptly described a decision-making conflict:

> I had a client who was getting a divorce and wanted a restraining order put into effect. When I spoke to her husband's attorney, he said, "Let's make that a mutual order." Even though my client was not physically abusing her husband, I had to recommend to her that she agree to the arrangement because I knew her husband could go into court and the court would order it. The client felt done to.
>
> When we went to court for the divorce hearing, the judge said that half-time visitation with the father was fine and insisted that the case should settle. I felt torn between the judge, who was making the decision and telling me this case should settle, and my client, who demanded that I let her get on the stand and tell her

story. I had to further weigh how what she wanted might antagonize the judge and hurt my future appearances before him.

External Pressures

Rather than feeling powerful ourselves, we usually are more aware of the power of others. Indeed, we often feel thwarted in our efforts to perform because we feel restrained by forces outside of our control. Having to encompass the agenda of a health maintenance organization, the politics of a university, or conflicting demands from a congregation leaves us feeling owned and controlled. Most important, the cooperation we need from clients to do our jobs leaves us uncomfortably dependent on their responsiveness to our efforts.

Frequently, we get angry with clients who challenge our power. They, too, struggle with our authority. Indeed, many boundary violations are initiated by clients who consciously or inadvertently try to reduce their greater vulnerability in the relationship by equalizing the power differential. A teacher described what happened when she allowed a student to violate the boundary:

> I had a student who challenged my authority. He would try to nail me with his questions. He was a ring leader who criticized everything I did quite openly. I watched his influence spread throughout the classroom, but I felt powerless to stop him. I kept defending myself by letting the class know what a good person I was, so that maybe they would do right by me. The hard part was that I didn't know how to evaluate the student. I lost my ability to be objective. I remember trying to read his papers and not being able to find the standards to assess his work. I was personally threatened because he was changing the rules.

Like the student in this example, some clients violate boundaries and initiate changing the rules. Sometimes they are ignorant about what is allowed. Other times their struggles with authority manifest in contests for control. While the credibility of professionals rides on our ability to be consistently dependable and reliable, clients' behavior is predictably erratic. After all, they are the ones in need and vulnerable to our influence.

When we are not aware of the ongoing risks and responsibilities inherent in the interaction, we may permit or even encourage the client's inappropriate behavior. If we misunderstand our role and do not feel we have the right to take charge, we may foster confusion about who is in charge or who has the power. If we feel helpless in relation to the client, we may not say no to unusual or inordinate demands. If we feel intimidated by the client's behavior or bewildered by the client's needs, we may abdicate our authority and become reactive to the client's control.

While struggles with authority are endemic to the professional-client relationship, we experience clients' demands as impediments to our work. Although these pressures are real, giving into them by dropping the leadership role and permitting the client's behavior to define the relationship leaves us feeling unduly victimized by the client. Staying externally focused on the obstacles that hinder our effectiveness feeds our internal agitation because we are reminded that we lack the control.

Internal Pressures

What we accomplish often determines our self-worth. The standards we use to measure ourselves further heighten the tension. A physician described her indoctrination into the medical community. She was told she was special and therefore had to pay for the privilege by being perfect. She observed, "You're told the first day of school that you're part of the upper 2% of the intellectual community and that's the last time you ever hear that. From then on you're told in obvious and quite subtle ways that you just don't measure up. If you just read a little more, cared a little more, or checked another lab test, you'd be a good doctor. You have to have the right answer. You have to be certain and you can't possibly fail."

While pressures may originate from outside sources, we internalize the prescription to be perfect and often drive ourselves relentlessly to meet this impossible goal. We erroneously believe that being perfect will help us reduce the tension we feel.

As professionals, we cannot control outcomes, predict accurately the behavior of clients, or regulate the external forces that impede our efforts. Our responsibility for living with dilemmas and having to make unpopular decisions, working with several constituencies and having to satisfy their varied demands, discerning the intentions of clients and having to differentiate their wishes from their needs, and being aware of the reality of human limitation but having to perform against the norm of excellence keeps us in a constant state of self-doubt. In this state, we can easily forget that we have more power than our clients.

THE DIALECTIC TENSION AND
THE MYTH OF CERTAINTY

Our unsureness runs counter to our image of a strong and qualified professional. As a doctor observed, "If you're a nurse or any lesser figure, you can't know as much as me. When an intensive care nurse calls with an observation about a patient and tactfully makes a recommendation, my ego rebels. Even though she's the person on the scene and involved with critical care patients five days a week, I'm the doctor. I'm the one who should make the decision. I've got to know more than she does." Since we equate being competent with feeling sure, not being certain disturbs our confidence and makes us apprehensive. Diverted from recognizing the power we hold and learning to come to terms with it, we struggle instead with unrealistic images of what we ought to be. Having power then becomes a product to be attained rather than a fact or condition of the relationship that exists regardless of the end result.

By trying to settle our inward struggle and calm our self-doubt, we fail to recognize the normalcy of the tension generated by the fact that, because we have greater power, we are in charge of what happens but we lack control over the outcome. As professionals, we live within the impossible binds of these two conflicting realities. We are expected to produce, but we are dependent on our clients. We are expected to be perfect, but we are aware of what could go wrong. We are obliged to keep the clients informed, but we are aware of the nuances, strategies, and political decisions that are beyond their comprehension. Such contradictions fill us with natural apprehensions.

Unfortunately, it is easy to misread our anxiety as a signal that something is wrong. Indeed, many of us misunderstand the origin of the tension and try to correct for it. Others of us may not even be conscious of its existence. It is there and we react out of our discomfort. We work to rid ourselves of whatever causes us to feel unsure and therefore less competent. Since we and our training institutions neither acknowledge nor normalize this tension, we are left stranded without the tools for understanding and handling it. As a consequence, we are prone to develop erroneous beliefs and to resort to more primitive ways of coping with the disquieting stress. These attempts to reduce or avoid our internal tension are dangerous because they change the boundaries that protect the space in the professional-client relationship.

FALSE ANSWERS

To relieve our uneasiness, we deny a part of our power by repositioning ourselves with our clients in two ways: (1) We try to be more in control by denying the significance of the professional-client relationship. (2) We try to be less in charge by denying the existence and significance of our greater authority. While each of these moves decreases the complexities and seemingly makes our work more manageable, this psychological shift of putting our comfort first undoes the ethos of care that binds us to the covenant with our clients. Furthermore, tightening or enlarging the space in the professional-client relationship undoes the controls on the relationship and thus paves the way for exploitation.

Denial of the Relationship

Operating within the professional-client relationship serves as a natural check and balance against the unmonitored exercise of power. Mindful of the asymmetry, some of us modulate our power according to the needs of our clients and the momentary circumstances. Many others of us, however, negate the importance of the professional-client relationship. We fear that the emotional aspects of the interaction could rattle our objectivity or interfere with the steadfastness of our conviction or purpose.

Seeking to distance ourselves from potentially upsetting conditions that could throw us off balance, we tend to objectify our clients and treat them as subjects or cases to be acted on rather than as persons with whom to engage. According to one attorney, "It's always a great temptation to treat the client's situation as mechanical or as something that is out there. The more you do that, the more control you have over the client. When you start to feel bad for the client, you don't have as much control." This and similar beliefs are common and even institutionalized in some of the professions. The fields of medicine and law are particularly vigilant in maintaining their focus on the medical or legal issues and, therefore, are susceptible to excluding the personhood of their clients.

Cultural Influence and Role Adaptation

Carved from the model of the traditionally patriarchal society, this stance presumes a hierarchial arrangement of dominance and submission between professional and client. An attorney observed, "Attorneys feel like it's just the attorneys who need to figure out a case. Clients, in a sense, become passive recipients. It takes too much time to have them involved. I know that many people feel horrible because their attorneys aren't telling them what is going on. Attorneys could say, 'Well, you don't need to understand that. That's what you hire me for.' And clients often feel too dumb to ask questions. I can really understand why they end up feeling tricked."

Performing according to the role prescribed for professionals allows us to legitimately reduce the tension by screening out the client or making the emotional component in the relationship tangential to the business at hand. By replacing our whole self with a role self, we feel more certain and in control. In that process, however, we negate who we are to ourselves. A law student described the process of numbing herself to feel like a lawyer:

> When I was studying for the bar exam, I realized that I had never empowered myself with the knowledge I had received in law school. What was important in school was giving the teachers the right answers, so what I learned was never mine. Since I saw this problem as a "woman's issue," I decided to change that around. As I continued to study for the test, I began to feel the shift. I was thinking like a lawyer. I didn't get what that meant until I realized that I was literally to give up everything from the neck down. You could not incorporate your feelings toward yourself or anything. If you chose to think like a lawyer, you had to give up everything else that had value in reality. I felt like I was almost choosing evil, and that felt horrible.

Splitting ourselves into pieces and rationalizing this behavior as necessary for maintaining our scientific objectivity supports the false dichotomy between mind and body. This belief system is further reinforced by our society, which both prescribes separate roles for men and women and gives a higher value to thinking than to feeling.

Danger to the Relationship

Divorcing parts of ourselves allows us to divorce the comparable parts of the client. By canceling out our own and the client's personhood, we, in effect, dismiss the relevance of the interpersonal connection. From this vantage point, we are vulnerable to denying our personal responsibility for the emotional impact of our actions on others. While being more in control helps us to feel more sure, when we are less aware of our impact we show less sensitivity to the imbalance engendered by the positions of caretaker and client. With less room for the client, the danger that we will misuse our power increases. For instance, one client shared how her therapist negated the significance of the professional-client relationship:

I had known and been in therapy with a psychiatrist for five years. He always told me how wonderful I was, how bright and unusual I was. He was the first person who affirmed me. I am a teacher. He consulted with the staff in my school district about problem children. One of my students was autistic. She had an IQ of about 70. No one could get her to respond. She was very passive-aggressive and nothing seemed to work.

A school conference was called with her parents. My psychiatrist, myself, and the school social worker were asked to attend. The father was an uptight manager and the mother was rosy, attractive, wide-eyed. My psychiatrist started working on the mother. "I bet you mother your daughter a lot," the psychiatrist contended. "I bet you let her get between you and your husband." I was appalled. He started throwing out all kinds of assumptions about what was wrong with this family. To me, they looked like fairly intelligent people who were dealing with a tough situation. It seemed to me that things had not been thoroughly explored. I don't even know if neurological testing had been done. Yet, my psychiatrist seemed to go straight for the heart.

I could tell the mother was getting seduced. She was crying, and the father looked overwhelmed. Finally, my psychiatrist said, "This is what I want you to do. You, Dad, should move in and share a bedroom with your daughter." In shock, the father asked, "What?" My psychiatrist continued, "You need to get between this daughter and her mother. You have to do this." The mother cried and agreed to the plan.

Several days later the father called me. He was enraged about what had happened. I suggested he check out his daughter's condition with someone else. I told him I thought his daughter needed to be examined elsewhere to see what she needed.

I'm sure both parents thought that I agreed with my psychiatrist. He had repeatedly said, "I've known this teacher for years." He brought in his relationship with me to get their trust. I couldn't say anything to my psychiatrist. I felt stunned and shocked, but I was intimidated by him. I had my self-image, as he had defined it, at stake. I felt very fragile. I felt like somehow I had to handle my relationship with him so that I could keep myself. I went to two more rotten conferences with my psychiatrist, and then I stopped going to the ones he attended. I still felt inadequate and I continued with him in therapy.

This psychiatrist minimized his therapeutic connection with the client, changed the limits, and violated the boundaries that protected the space between them. He divorced himself from the relationship and seemingly took no responsibility for the emotional impact of his actions. Unencumbered by the complexities around him, he then proceeded to use his power manipulatively and outside the relational context. Rather than giving primacy to his relationship with the teacher as his client, he muddied the association and moved the boundary by becoming her consultant as well. Rather than helping the parents to feel effective by working with them to find a solution to their problem, he took over the family without placing any restrictions on his role. Rather than respecting the teacher's relationship with the parents and operating within that established framework, he both used and discounted her position as his client. As if what he did made no difference to her, he relegated her to the position of an assistant and unilaterally changed her status both as a teacher and as a client. Rather than being sensitive to the impact of his consultation on his client, he did not attend to the repercussions of his pronouncements for either his client or the family. Moreover, he assumed no responsibility for the influence of his personal power as he forthrightly advised a vulnerable family to engage in symbolically incestuous behavior. His denial of the significance of all these relationships revealed that the reactions of others to his power were inconsequential to him. Rather than respecting the power differential and assuming responsibility for his impact on others, he capitalized on the differential and used his greater authority to achieve more control and seize more power.

When as professionals we deny the relationship, we operate outside of it, thereby wiping out the boundary that protects our clients from our misuse of power. In turn, clients frequently compensate and inappropriately assume the responsibility for the relationship that we have abandoned. If something goes wrong, they question themselves rather than us, which, in effect, relieves us of all responsibility. By placing the burden on themselves, clients keep us unaware of our impact and spare us the discomfort and tension we might otherwise feel. In the example just described, the teacher never challenged the psychiatrist's subversion of their therapeutic relationship. As a result, she absorbed the fallout from the psychiatrist's negative impact on the student's parents.

Denial of Our Authority

Many of us are comfortable operating within the professional-client relationship only when we refuse to acknowledge our greater authority. We believe that the tension we feel results from our superior status in the relationship. Since having more power implies its possible misuse, we try to dissociate ourselves from the threat we pose in having power over others. Worried that "taking charge" might ruin or dismantle the emotional connection with our clients, we divorce ourselves from our authority in order not to alienate them. "I used not to be able to draw the line," said an attorney. "I couldn't say hard things effectively, and I let conversations with clients go on too long. I didn't want to offend anyone. I didn't want someone to go away mad." By avoiding taking charge in the professional-client relationship, professionals try to reduce the tension from the pushes and pulls that are endemic to the connection.

Cultural Influence and Role Adaptation

The decision to assume an egalitarian posture is often made in reaction to a hierarchial model. Indeed, the ideology of equality is the underpinning of our democracy, many religious denominations, and some feminist organizations. A former cleric described how he had used this philosophy to blind himself to the impact of his authority:

> My own ideology was very much the ideology that is reinforced in the church. I believed in a shared ministry. I believed that people in the church should be friends. I didn't want to set myself apart as superior. I felt that the minister needed to be part of the group. Having your primary friends be outside of the congregation didn't fit with this ideal picture of friendship and community. Therefore, my best friends were members of the congregation. Now I know that each person's participation in the church is influenced by the one-to-one relationship with the minister. If the minister is best friends with one or two or three people, that's going to have an influence on the life of the whole congregation. It makes an in-group and an out-group, and things like that are really deadly for a church.

A therapist described how she used a version of feminist ideology as the basis for negating her greater power and for undoing the boundaries in the therapist-client relationship:

> Having no boundaries was normalized within the therapeutic community to which I belonged. The party line was that power was a male construct and that women clients had been hurt and oppressed by male therapists. The women who influenced me

distorted the word "feminist." They believed that "feminist" therapists, who were really aware, needed to form a new model that
erased the hierarchy and false divisions between therapist and
client. I had clients whom I liked and I made them friends. I told
them all kinds of things about my personal life. I probably used
them to gratify my own needs. I dismissed any problems that I had
with what I was doing as a product of my patriarchal conditioning.
Since I wanted to be a good feminist, I complied with the current
behavioral standards.

In both these examples, an ideology institutionalized as a counter-
force supported the professionals' denial of their greater authority, allowing them to substitute the pretense of equality for the reality of the
power differential. When we displace the authority in our role onto an
ideology and behave according to something outside of us, we abdicate
our personal responsibility for managing our greater power inside the
relationship.

In addition to following the scripts of our personal ideologies, many
of us are insecure and do not feel personally empowered. We seek to
calm our apprehension so that we can feel stronger and more certain.
Unsure of what is permissible and fearful of the anger we might encounter from our clients, we hold back on fully exercising our greater authority and fail to take on the full dimensions of the professional role. "I
think you're in a role," said a minister, "a role that you have to live up to.
And there might be certain things about yourself that just don't fit. Most
of my life I have run away from authority and wanted someone else to
be responsible. I didn't feel worthy to have any kind of authority, and so
I've been very passive for most of my life. My approach to the ministry
has been pretty passive, too."

Indeed, the professional role demands more of the self than we would
otherwise express. It requires that we use our greater power to take
charge of the conditions that keep our clients safe in the professional-
client relationship. Holding ourselves back from assuming this responsi-

bility makes us passive participants in a relationship that presumes and requires our active leadership. While our not taking charge avoids the discomfort of taking stands that may be unpopular with others, our clients continue to see us as having more power and look to us for direction. When we do not act within the framework of our role, our inconsistency and unpredictable behavior make the boundaries in the relationship ambiguous and our clients become confused.

Danger to the Relationship

Refusing our greater authority spares us the uneasiness of exposing who we are to our clients. As long as nothing threatens the balance between us, we can maintain an uneasy peace with them. When we are pushed to assume our full authority, however, we feel the tension and frequently placate our clients, which has the effect of putting them in charge of us. When we change priorities and goals, placing our need for our clients' goodwill first, we cannot make decisions from a solid base. Being more concerned with our clients' approval than with doing what is best for them can even skew the advice we give.

When we fail to set limits, we take less charge of the boundaries that protect the space in the relationship. The vacuum created allows clients to determine the parameters and to enlarge the space between us. Without our direction or leadership, there is no check and balance on the reality of our clients' expectations. As a result, clients often fill the void with their own agendas. Our refusal to accept the authority that comes with our role while actively participating in the relationship thus lays the groundwork for inappropriate behavior.

A client shared what happened when her attorney abdicated his responsibility and placed no limits on her behavior. When he later reacted to the out-of-control situation, he cut off psychologically from the client and rigidly held the reins, which both confused her and left her feeling orphaned.

I hired an attorney for my divorce. I knew him from church. He was a deacon and seemed to be a Christian person with values. Because of these connections, I felt comfortable putting my trust in him. He told me that I should not hesitate to call him with any problem or question. "Even if it's on the weekend," he said, "if there are problems and something happens, call me at home." He was always encouraging me to keep in touch with him. I felt he was trying to be helpful, almost like he was trying to counsel me along the way. He knew I was in a lousy situation, but he was willing to help me work it through.

I was in tough circumstances. I had worked as a cook before I sustained an injury. I wound up in the hospital for a month because of anxiety and depression. I had been a home health aide but had not kept up my certification. Occasionally, I did grocery store checkout. Other than that I had nothing. I had no skills so I went back to school. I didn't have a job, and I was trying to support my three young children and maintain a household.

When I first hired him, my attorney said that because I had no money and no job or other source of income, a lien against my home was a possibility. He reassured me that this was only a formality. I didn't want to take a chance of my children or me ending up on the street so I told him no. He kept telling me that everything would work out fine. I just remember feeling desperate as problems piled up.

Not thinking upfront that this was going to cost a lot of money, I would call him. And he didn't remind me that the clock was ticking. I didn't get a bill for six months. When it came, he indicated that the fee would be about $5,000. I felt angry and told him I wanted this divorce finalized. He continued to encourage my calls. I felt that if I let him know more about my problems and concerns, he would hurry up and get things finished. I needed closure at that point. There had been far too much abuse.

Two months later the divorce was final. Everything was split. I had to give my former husband a mortgage for his portion of the equity in the house. My attorney asked me to come to his office to review the decree. I said I wanted to appeal the decision, as I felt the settlement was not equitable or fair. He told me the judge's decision was final. I then asked about bankruptcy, since I had incurred such a heavy debt load. He told me I couldn't file bankruptcy. I found out later that wasn't true. I could have appealed and I could have filed bankruptcy.

At this same meeting, he had a pile of papers for me to sign. I said, "What is this that I'm signing?" He said, "They are just the final papers." I asked, "Well, do I need to know anything about them?" He said, "No, we just have to sign them and turn them back in." I didn't know the law. I was just a layperson. I believed he knew what was best and would not lie to me.

What I didn't realize was that one of the papers was a lien against my house. At that time, I had $10,000 worth of bills—which included my student loans—no spousal maintenance, and no pension. I used the child support to afford the house payments. I was living on charge cards so that I could buy shoes for my kids and gas for my car to get back and forth to school. I wasn't able to pay much on my attorney's bill. Eventually, he wrote me a letter threatening foreclosure on my home unless I paid his entire bill. I had to put my house on the market because I had no money.

Worst of all, before he would release the lien on my house so it could be sold, he coerced me into signing a paper stipulating that I would not bring any action against him in the future. It was a catch-22. Either way I lost. I had put my trust in this person. I told him time and time again that I was putting my life in his hands. I paid him to work in my best interest and I trusted that he was doing that. Now I know that I was giving him permission to slaughter me. By taking my home, he took the only thing I had left besides my kids.

Even though he is a deacon at church, I won't acknowledge him. Sometimes he tries to say something to me and I won't answer. I'd like to scream, "You profess to be so holy, yet you'd screw your mother if you had the chance!" I don't owe him anything. I paid my bill!

This attorney clearly was uncomfortable with exercising his authority. He left the boundaries of the relationship undefined and placed no limits on his availability. In response to his needs and his invitation, his client innocently defined and structured the relationship. When his generosity made him uneasy, the attorney took his greater power out of hiding and used it to extricate himself.

The motive for his generosity is suspect. Based on the client's story, it is not clear whether he made himself available because he was concerned about her welfare or so that he could get paid more. Unfortunately, the client paid a high price for his deceit. After having encouraged her dependency, he changed the rules and used his power punitively when he sent her a six-month-old bill. Pretending she did not have to sign a lien against her house for his services, he again deceived her when she signed the final divorce papers. When he realized he might not get his money, he lied and told her she could not file bankruptcy. Ultimately, he took her house but still tried to maintain an amiable connection when he saw her in church. This attorney consistently opted to be dishonest in order to maintain his comfort and attend to his self-interests in the relationship. Even today, he tries to make contact with his ex-client in church to reduce the tension between them. Again and again, this client was punished and hurt because of the attorney's reluctance to assert his authority appropriately.

When we deny our authority, our clients become the object of our struggle with power. While divorcing ourselves from our authority makes us more comfortable, it skews the power differential and falsely positions us and our clients as equal. From this vantage point, no one is in charge or responsible. The danger to clients who are vulnerable and in the less powerful position is obvious. We professionals still have the control even though we pretend otherwise. By using it in covert ways, we manipulate our clients according to our self-interests, as happened to the woman in the example just described.

While we may feel less vulnerable in taking a laissez-faire posture, the tension we resist does not disappear. It merely goes underground and resurfaces whenever we become worried about our welfare.

THE LARGER RESPONSIBILITY

The difficulty we professionals have in owning our full power is the primary psychological gateway that ushers in and permits boundary violations. By negating both our personal significance and our authority, we disturb the power differential in the professional-client relationship. Our mythology that being certain internally makes us powerful and competent externally and our belief that tension means something is wrong propel us toward the goals of being perfect, being right, winning, knowing more, not being questioned, being liked, and being acceptable. By unconsciously placing our comfort first, we make our clients' needs secondary to our own.

Boundary violations grow out of our struggles with power and our negation of its significance. The extent to which violations happen suggests that our difficulty accepting and working within the natural asymmetry of the professional-client relationship is common. To incorporate both the professional-client relationship and our greater authority, we have to forego our goal of comfortability. We have to recognize and accept our larger responsibility for ourselves by becoming aware of and tolerating the dynamic tension that exists when both realities are acknowledged. If we accept the significance of the relationship, we have to control and limit our power; we have to modify it within the context of the relationship to fit each client's needs. If we accept our authority, we have to alter our position of feigned equality; we have to concede that the professional-client relationship is not democratic, that we have more power than our clients, and that we make intentional choices that influence their lives. Either way is a challenge.

While the power differential is a secular reality, how we choose to handle it reflects the depth of our commitment to the covenant we make with our clients. Indeed, our willingness to monitor our self-interests reaffirms the sacredness of the connection between us. The self-discipline involved reminds us that we are fundamentally guided by the spiritual values that underscore the relationship.

Only when we realize that there is no escape—that we, too, have to surrender a part of ourselves to these realities—can we acknowledge the boundaries that protect the integrity of the professional-client connection. We have to learn to live with the dichotomy between the power that puts us in charge and the relationship that keeps us controlled, the duality of feeling powerful at one level and powerless at another, and the incongruence of being autonomous while being restrained. As professionals, our willingness to live in the eye of the storm is our most profound challenge.

IV

BOUNDARY VIOLATIONS:
THE MISUSE OF POWER

A S PROFESSIONALS, WE STRUGGLE to accept our limitations. We would rather not see that we are fallible human beings who make mistakes. To separate ourselves out from the more extreme offenders, we selectively blind ourselves to our own misbehavior and acknowledge only the worst and most blatant violations of other professionals in our respective fields. This "us and them" posture is dangerous; we can miss early warning signals that could alert us to the trouble ahead.

Detecting a boundary violation is difficult because it is a process rather than a single event. It grows like a cancer beneath the surface of the relationship's legitimate purpose and is hard to recognize until it emerges as a serious, blatant problem. Since each violation is shaped by the context of the relationship, violations resist classification, which makes them even more difficult to pinpoint. Some are more damaging than others. Some are more acknowledged within the professions as harmful, while others are dismissed as communication problems or differences in the professional's and the client's perceptions.

Most important, the size and visibility of boundary violations are masked because they happen within the framework of the professional-client relationship. This protective cover helps clients and professionals alike to normalize situations that damage the covenant between them. While violations fall on a continuum from minor mistakes to major transgressions, they all share the same characteristics. Learning to recognize the similarities gives us a map for deciphering potentially risky situations.

FREQUENCY OF BOUNDARY VIOLATIONS

Violating the boundaries of the professional-client relationship is a common occurrence. Whether the violation is inadvertent or premeditated, the initial decisions we make about how to manage the relationship have critical ramifications. What we do can appear harmless. For instance, we fail to hold our limits about the duration or frequency of counseling sessions or we flirt with a student. We fear saying no to an intimidating or contemptuous parishioner or we ask a patient who is a stockbroker about a stock option rather than searching the community for an independent broker. While seemingly innocuous, such initial moves muddy the base of the professional-client connection in that the professional's needs are placed ahead of the client's needs. A client described how easily and naturally this switch happened when she met her new therapist for the first time. Remembering the relationship with her old therapist, she said:

> My first counselor never talked about her personal life. She set boundaries for me. When she was about to leave town and we ended therapy, I asked if I could write her. I had a history of addictive relationships. She knew that writing her would stimulate

a false belief that we could continue our relationship outside of therapy. She didn't want to hurt me that way. So she said that it would be better for me if I didn't write her. She had good boundaries, but I didn't realize it at the time. I thought she was rejecting me and shutting me out.

The first time I saw my new therapist, she did something that wasn't right. When I told her who my former therapist was, she got excited and exclaimed, "I know her! We are really good friends." Immediately I thought, "My old therapist never would have shared that information." It was such a little thing but I realized the new therapist was insecure and that I could manipulate her. I began to plot how I could continue a relationship with my original therapist by how I managed the relationship with this new woman.

The reference made by the client's new counselor seems outwardly benign. The therapist probably believed that by telling this client about her personal friendship with the other therapist, she could help the client to feel more comfortable with her. Even with the best of intentions, though, accidents happen. In fact, it seldom occurs to us professionals that such casual responses could initiate a boundary violation. Yet, many clients, in recounting their experiences, can trace the origins of a professional transgression to similar comments. Rather than being the exception, these deceptively small and simple mistakes happen frequently. Often we do not see the danger until we are loudly awakened by the repercussions and aftershocks that occur.

BOUNDARY VIOLATION DEFINED

Boundaries are the limits that allow for a safe connection based on the client's needs. When these limits are altered, what is allowed in the relationship becomes ambiguous. Such ambiguity is often experienced as an intrusion into the sphere of safety. The pain from a violation is frequently delayed, and

the violation itself may not be recognized or felt until harmful consequences emerge.

Boundary violations are acts that breach the core intent of the professional-client association. They happen when professionals exploit the relationship to meet personal needs rather than client needs. Changing that fundamental principle undoes the covenant, altering the ethos of care that obliges professionals to place clients' concerns first. In fact, all of the boundaries in a professional-client relationship exist in order to protect this core understanding.

A student described her experience with a teacher who violated the boundary by using her to do his work.

I was a bright student from Columbia and transferred to the state university to be with my husband. I knew I was more advanced than the other students. I wanted to take a particular course that was open to both graduates and undergraduates. The teacher said he was sorry but the class was full. However, he needed a teaching assistant. I remember that he said, "I'll tell you what I'll do. If you'll be my teaching assistant and grade everyone else's papers, you can take the class for graduate credit." I remember thinking, "This is corrupt. This is rotten. On the other hand, if I'm going to get my degree, I have to have this course." So he would hand out the topics, I would hand in my paper, which he always returned marked with an A, and then I would grade the other students' work.

The last week of class I asked him when he wanted me to take my final exam. He said, "Don't bother." It was nice to be treated as someone so special that I could be excused from the test, but it also made me uncomfortable. I felt cheated. He let himself off the hook as a teacher and made me a co-conspirator by letting me off the hook as a student. My failure to take the final exam and the dishonesty associated with my education have left me with a real contempt for my degree.

In this case, the student innocently approached the teacher about taking his class. She knew he had the power to let her in or to keep her out. She assumed that the relationship was based on the teacher doing for the student. However, the inherent ethos of care between them was changed into a bargain. Rather than placing her needs first, the teacher seized the opportunity to lessen his own workload. He undermined her interests as a student and used her advanced skills to grade the other students' papers. Changing this boundary altered the reality about whose needs came first. However, since he was the teacher and she the student, the official story reads that he did her a favor both by allowing her to take the class and by excusing her from the final exam.

Ambiguity is reflected in the student's confusion. She felt both special and used. Aware of the dishonesty in his offer, however, she registered the intrusion into the sphere of safety between them as she let herself acknowledge his motives. "This is corrupt," she said. "This is rotten." At the same time, she was coerced into the position of an indentured servant. "If I'm going to get my degree," she said, "I have to have this course." Forced to compromise her values, she did not recognize the insidious nature of the violation until she described the contempt she now feels about her degree.

THE CHARACTERISTICS OF
A BOUNDARY VIOLATION

Since boundary violations are disguised and hidden under the aegis of the professional-client relationship, they are difficult to discern. Therefore, the ingredients that comprise a boundary violation are buried underground. In every story of a violation, however, four motifs surface: a reversal of roles, a secret, a double bind, and an indulgence of professional privilege. As integral parts of the whole, these four characteristics are interconnected and become a dynamic system that has a wayward life of its own.

The Reversal of Roles

In a boundary violation, the professional and the client switch places and the client becomes the caretaker. The professional structures the inside of the relationship according to his or her needs. Having reversed roles, the professional now looks to the client for gratification. A client reflected on how she took care of a cleric. "I made him feel good," she said. "I told him how important he was, how much I loved him. I would write him letters. It was obvious that I adored him. That must have felt really nice for him. We all want to feel good and I know that I made him feel special."

The professional who places any portion of his or her needs first in the relationship twists the ethos of care by assuming the primary and dependent position. Giving priority to his or her own concerns, however, is often an unconscious act—one concealed even from the professional. Frequently, the behavior is justified by the professional who contends that his or her actions are for the client's benefit. A client described her compliance with a physician's schedule:

> Whenever I saw this doctor, he was always two hours late for my appointment. I would spend half a day waiting. His secretary would say to me, "You know, Dr. M. responds to people on the basis of need. So when people come in and need more time, they get more time." I remember that I used to call his office and ask how late he was running. Even though I waited at home until he was ready, when I came in I would still have to wait hours. I would never say to Dr. M., "You know it pisses me off. I have valuable things to do too and it makes me feel like next to nothing when I have to stand around for two hours in your tiny waiting room." But he was all I had. He was my lifeline at this point. The thought of finding another doctor was beyond me.

In this example, the client took care of the physician by (1) adjusting her life to comply with the idiosyncracy of his schedule, (2) not bothering the physician with her feelings, and (3) silently enduring his extreme tardiness. The physician disguised his inability to manage time and excused his behavior by claiming that he was controlled by his clients' needs. This logic, in effect, placed the client in charge of the relationship and makes the physician an innocent victim of whatever he decided was warranted for his other clients.

Even though the client becomes the caretaker in a boundary violation, the professional does not give up the control. The professional still defines the parameters of the relationship, determining whose needs will come first and who will meet them. The decision to give priority to his or her concerns is made unilaterally and without the client's full knowledge or consent.

The client first experiences the reversal of roles as a shift in status. Because the professional looks to the client to meet his or her needs, the client is assigned a new power. Not knowing the real reason behind the change, the client follows the professional's lead. A client who had sustained a head injury felt the change in status when her attorney took her to lunch:

> My attorney was going to be my mentor. He would come and get me and we would go out to some fancy place for lunch. Even though I liked the restaurants, I felt awkward. I was used to eating at McDonald's. My attorney told me he loved me as a daughter. He used to joke a lot and say, "You're just beautiful. You're the most beautiful girl." I knew I wasn't beautiful but it seemed like something a father might say to a daughter. He got overly enthusiastic about things. That was just his way.

When the roles are initially reversed, some clients feel elevated in the eyes of the professional. Like a mood-altering drug, the change in status from what they expected feels wonderful. It creates a natural high. Clients mistakenly believe that feeling special stems from who they are as people. They feel validated and chosen. In reality, they are special only because of their ability to minister to the professional's needs. One client described her euphoric state after her minister began a slow seduction by rubbing her neck and telling her how much he valued and liked her:

> I didn't walk out of his office. I floated out. I remember going to the store, trying on clothes and everything looked good on me. I never had such high self-esteem in my whole life. After that experience with my minister, I wanted to look nice every time we got together. I chose my clothing with care and made sure my nails were polished. I probably became obsessional about it. It was almost a relief when he left the church, and I could go to services without worrying about my appearance.

For other clients, reversing the roles creates a downward spiral. Although assigned a new power, the client still feels like a scapegoat for the professional's anger and abuse. Unable to explain the change, the client feels responsible for what has gone wrong. More concerned with winning the professional's favor than with meeting their own needs, clients try to "be good" to melt away the professional's disapproval. A student described his relationship with his research advisor:

> I've always felt insecure in terms of my abilities, that in some way I didn't legitimately belong in this field. My professor knew that I had this Achilles' heel. When I would give an opinion, he would say, "You don't know what you're talking about." Since he wasn't specific about what I had done wrong, I would start thinking about my deficits from the past. Whenever I would argue with him, he would throw a temper tantrum like a child. "You're snowing me!" he would yell. "You're trying to pull the wool over my eyes. How long have you done research compared with me?" If I went to see him with a question, he would talk for three to four hours. He would get a high from hearing himself speak. It was self-stimulating. If you agreed with what he said in these marathon sessions, he would finally let you go. Other times he would stop in the middle of a sentence and say, "Tell me what I just said." If you couldn't remember verbatim, he would say, "That is not what I

said. You've got to stop me when you don't understand." I was always afraid. I couldn't predict what he might do. I think he needed to have total power and total control over me. For me to have any power of my own was threatening to him.

Changing the client's status by reversing the roles creates a new reality. The feeling of safety necessary for learning is replaced with terror. The function of the learning environment for the student is transformed into a platform for the aggrandizement of the teacher. Instead of the professional taking care of the client, the client has to continue to take care of the professional in order to get what she or he needs. In this story, the teacher used his power to emotionally abuse the student. The student had to endure the abuse in order to receive both the teacher's general knowledge about the subject and the teacher's specific approval for his research design.

As with this student, most clients have little power or control over the fundamental redefinition of the relationship and the change in status. Even if the client initiates or accedes to the reversal of roles, the inherent asymmetry of the relationship makes the client an unequal participant. The pretense of normality, however, obscures the client's vision. Since the professional continues to perform his or her functions, the client takes care of the professional while believing the professional is taking care of her or him. As in the story *Alice in Wonderland*, these dual realities distort the relationship and turn it upside down and inside out. Reversing the roles blurs the boundary between professional and client and dismantles the shared understanding that allows clients to feel safe in the relationship.

The Secret

In a boundary violation, critical knowledge or behavior is kept from the client. Concealing information that is potentially detrimental to the client's well-being erodes the honesty of the connection and pollutes the trust that is necessary for the client's protection. Inviting a student of environmental conservation on a field trip in hopes of a sexual liaison, befriending a wealthy client for the purpose of enhancing one's own social status, and prematurely terminating a patient so that the professional can take advantage of the patient's skills for his or her business are examples of secrets that are destructive to the primary intent of the professional-client relationship. The withholding of information gives the secret holder an unfair advantage in the relationship. He or she can gain the cooperation of the client to achieve certain goals without having to disclose the true motive or full agenda. Without the critical knowledge required for a reasonable choice on the client's part, the client is manipulated into participating unknowingly in the professional's plan. A nurse described her experience with a physician who accelerated a medical procedure so that he could get to a dinner party on time:

> When a mom comes into the hospital to have her baby, we sometimes use Pitocin. Pitocin is used to stimulate or induce labor by causing uterine contractions. We start the intravenous infusion slowly. Sometimes women refuse this artificial procedure. I remember one mom who clearly said that she wanted to give birth naturally and without any interference. The doctor told her all the medical reasons why that was not a good idea. He started her on Pitocin.
>
> The truth of the matter was that he was in a hurry. He had told me outside her room that he had to get to a social function that night and that we needed to "push the pit." He really meant that I was to increase the rate of Pitocin infusion in order to get her delivered as soon as possible. The mom didn't have any idea what was happening. She went along with her doctor's recommendation not knowing she'd been conned.

As in this story, secrets tend to produce three-person triangles of deceit. Here the nurse and the physician excluded the patient from the decision while supporting her erroneous belief that the procedure was necessary for medical reasons. The nurse knew the physician's real motive and felt caught between her concern for the patient and her subservient role in relation to the physician. The physician knew the patient was ignorant and that the nurse was obligated to follow his orders.

Such intrigue creates a subsystem of fraudulent alliances and destructive divisions that distorts the space between professional and client. In a boundary violation, the presence of secrets functions either (1) to separate the client from the professional while deceitfully maintaining the pretense of a common endeavor (as in the example just described) or (2) to falsely join the client and professional against those who are on the outside and do not know the secret.

A psychology intern described how her supervisor tried to use her as an accomplice in his secret plan to hurt another employee:

> My supervisor was angry at an employee who had rejected his sexual advances. He had accosted her and she was afraid for her safety. He was looking for a way to get rid of her. He wanted me to lead a therapy group with her, tape the sessions, and bring the tapes into my supervision session with him. He wanted secretly to gain information about her work that he could use to justify her termination. He pretended that he was doing it for my education. He also asked me to do it for her.
>
> When I refused, he said, "You should be more concerned about what she is doing with clients. You're interfering with the process of the help that she needs." We had a second confrontation and I still refused. This time he said, "You either tape those sessions or get out of here." As I went to leave, he said, "If you walk out, you had better not come back."

More important than the content of the secret, though, is its effect on both the professional and the client. A secret splits rather than strengthens the bond of trust. It protects behaviors that are not legitimate to the intent and purpose of the professional-client relationship by restricting the client's access to knowing. Because the professional acts out of the secret rather than out of regard for the client's need, a part of the professional's self is not available to engage with the client. This invisible withholding subtly disrupts and blocks the natural flow of the relationship. The partial disappearance of the professional confounds and confuses the client. A married client who was having an affair did not know that her therapist was also counseling her lover. She described her bewilderment before she discovered the secret:

> I kept trying to talk about the affair. In the beginning of therapy, we had spent a lot of time on my feelings about my lover. But when I broke off the affair, I noticed we didn't talk about him anymore. The therapist focused instead on my family of origin. I still had contact with this lover in other situations that were harrowing experiences for me. I wanted to talk about these episodes. She always seemed to change the subject. I felt like she was minimizing it and that I couldn't talk about it. Sometimes I would think, "I'm paying for this session. I want to talk about this man." It bothered me for months, but it never clicked in my head to broach the subject with her.

Since this client could only see part of the picture, her perception of reality was altered. The presence of a secret alongside the client's authentic need undermined the client's psychotherapy and mental health in that a dual but clandestine agenda had been created. The client did not know to which agenda she was responding. Because the official order of business continued, the secret was naturally camouflaged. As a result, reality testing was incomplete and greatly diminished, since the client was unable to adequately categorize information, predict the future, and respond appropriately.

A parishioner described her experience with a cleric whom she saw for spiritual support:

> He gave me a piece in the Bible to read and told me to write my reactions in a journal. I was supposed to read my journal to him in

our sessions. He was studying sexuality and spirituality, and he told me that he was considering an advanced degree in sexology. He told me about his fidelity to his wife and that he would never have intercourse with anyone else. Implicitly, his disclosure meant that he was safe. I was not to be afraid.

So I read to him from my journal. Sometimes he would hint that a particular Bible passage might make me feel sexual. When that happened, I knew I was doing it right. I was so impressed because he was a minister who was open to talking about sexuality. Yet, when I shared with him, he would get this weird smile like he was enjoying it and his eyes would glaze over. Somehow I was being a good girl and doing what I was told. I felt real important.

Yet, anytime I was reluctant to share the sexually explicit thoughts I had, he would shame me about being uptight. I would feel embarrassed or think that telling him was inappropriate. I would feel there must be something wrong with me that I couldn't talk about it. I would think, "I'm not as free and open as this wonderful person here." Instead of feeling good about myself, I felt more ashamed. Now I know he used his response to manipulate me into sharing my private sexual thoughts with him.

In this example, the client's perceptions of reality were distorted by the dual agenda. She could not determine whether the minister's positive reaction to her sharing indicated his approval or, rather, a sexual response to her thoughts. When she resisted sharing, she could not tell whether her reluctance was a healthy reaction to his voyeurism or revealed an abnormal response and lack of comfort with sexuality on her part. Unable to access the secret of his motivation, she was vulnerable to his misdirection and confused as to the basis of her intuitive responses.

Secrets are not always invisible to the client. As a matter of fact, the client, as well as the professional, may initiate the transgression that produces the secret. Even if the secret is initiated by the client, the professional's decision to collude is central to the progression of the violation. Since it is the professional's responsibility to manage the relationship, permitting the secret to occur and to remain unaddressed leads to the corruption that damages the primary purpose and intent of the association. A psychiatrist described her experience with a client who left her artwork with her for safekeeping:

> This client was suicidal. She told me that her fear of being abandoned was a major issue in her life. She was severely depressed but had no insurance to pay for hospitalization and no money to pay me. She decided to go to California to regroup.
>
> One day she walked into my waiting room unannounced, carrying five of her paintings. When I came out of my office, she jumped up and said, "My plane is leaving in an hour. I brought these paintings to give you." I didn't want to accept them, but I didn't want her to miss her flight, so I said quickly, "I'll keep your paintings for you in a safe place. When you come back, we'll talk about it some more." The client responded, "You've done so much for me, and I know I won't ever be able to pay you enough. These paintings are very important. I've been working on them for the past seven years. Even though I'm just making it, I know that painting these pictures has been keeping me alive." Then she dashed out the door.
>
> Now she keeps calling me from out of town and telling me she doesn't want to go on living. Since I have her paintings, I feel obligated to deal with her. She has a history of suicide attempts. I'm afraid that if I return her paintings, she will feel rejected.

In this example, the client initiated the secret by giving her artwork to the psychiatrist. Unclear about whether the artwork was a form of payment or a gift, the psychiatrist felt dishonest because she had accepted something that did not seem to belong to her and was not part of their professional contract. She felt imprisoned by the client.

As in many boundary violations, the real secret, however, was not about the content but rather about the motive or intent of the initiator. In this instance, the real secret was not that the client had turned over her paintings but rather that she had "bought" the psychiatrist and made her responsible for her life. By agreeing to the client's terms, the psychiatrist completed the secret. Even though the client took advantage of the psychiatrist's fiduciary obligation, the psychiatrist's position of greater authority made her ultimately responsible for the transgression.

The Double Bind

In a boundary violation, the client is caught in a conflict of interest. Any direction he or she moves is potentially hazardous. Any attempt to resolve the dilemma places him or her at risk for a loss of some kind. Consequently, the range of plausible options for handling the difficulty is severely limited and the client feels unable to overcome the impasse. A client described the bind he faced when his physician asked him to be the coauthor of some articles:

> I was in a support group at the hospital for depression. A well-known writer, I hated giving my name because someone would always say, "Oh, I've read your books." I didn't want to be singled out. I just wanted to be there for myself and not for anyone else.
>
> After one of the meetings, the doctor in charge of the group showed me some articles she had written about depression. She said I might find the information useful, but she didn't stop there. She went on to ask me to critique the material and suggested we might collaborate later on a book. At first I felt flattered. When I later realized she was using me, I felt furious. I would like to have told her how angry I was, but I couldn't. I still needed the group and I didn't want to make her mad.

In this example, the client experienced possible loss on more than one level. He felt unable to say no; to refuse the physician's offer would have looked like he was refusing her help for his condition. Furthermore, if he had said no, she might have felt rejected and punished him in some way. Being viewed as noncompliant and therefore uncooperative could even have affected his treatment. To accept her offer, however, would have been equally hazardous. Agreeing to be used would have undermined his struggle to be valued for who he is rather than for servicing others. Furthermore, if he had acquiesced, he, not the physician, would have felt responsible for the decision. Abandoning what he needed for himself while feeling trapped and responsible might have locked him further into depression and despair.

Boundary violations place clients in untenable binds. Since they are highly dependent on the professional, clients feel both trapped inside the relationship and bound by their perceived inability to move independently. They are tied both by what they need from the professional and by their fear of being without the relationship. If they give up the relationship, they lose the professional's needed expertise. If they stay in the relationship, they lose a part of their personhood. A client described her dilemma with a urologist who was insensitive to her pain:

> When I was 19, I tried to have sexual intercourse. It was very painful so I went to see the urologist who had performed surgery on my kidney when I was three. At that time, he had fought against other doctors who were recommending urinary diversion, which would mean that I would have had to wear a urine-collecting bag the rest of my life. He had said, "I'll operate a hundred times on her before I do that and make her life miserable." He was like a hero and I felt totally indebted to him. He had told my mom I might have some problems with sexual intercourse that might necessitate more surgery.
>
> I decided to go back to him because he understood my history. He discounted my concern about sex. Instead, he wanted to perform a voiding cystogram and injected dye into my bladder to see how much I could retain. I always ask doctors, "How is this going to affect me? Is it going to hurt?" And usually doctors tell me what instruments they are going to put into me and how long a procedure will take. He wouldn't tell me anything. Even though he

injected dye through my urethra with a tube, he said, "Let's see where this pain is" and stuck his finger into my vagina.

It was weird and totally awful. The procedure lasted 20 minutes. I kept asking him how much longer it would take, which made me look neurotic. I was crying the whole time because it was so painful. Never once did he warn me about the pain or ask if I was okay.

When the exam was over, I was very upset. He calmly told me that everything looked good. Later his nurse told me to make another appointment. I could only nod because I was still in pain, crying, and holding this suppository in my urethra. I was too scared to do anything else. I felt completely dehumanized. I think he has problems with pain and honesty. Not once did he look at me to see how I was doing. He was only interested in my urethra.

In this example, the client felt trapped. Highly dependent on the physician's judgment, she agreed to the test. Had she stopped it she would have deprived herself of information she believed was necessary to diagnose her condition. By letting it continue, however, she hurt herself by enduring both the pain and the physician's insensitivity. Either way she felt like a coward. Interrupting the procedure meant she was a "chicken" or a crybaby. Continuing it meant she was a wimp who was submissive to others.

In a boundary violation, the double bind always contains an implied threat. Clients feel paralyzed by the danger. On the one hand, feeling indebted to the professional for his or her help, they worry that they will betray the relationship if they comment on the violation. The guilt, along with the real fear of possible abandonment by the professional, blocks them from taking action. On the other hand, their continuing participation in a violation risks their integrity, because they fail to give credence to their inner voice that says something is wrong. In fact, their dishonesty about how they really feel unites them with the dishonesty of the professional who is placing his or her needs first. As they abandon themselves by violating their own boundaries and compromising their needs, they lose respect for themselves. They join the professional in placing their needs second. Their admission of this collusion costs too much to tell. Frozen by their fear, clients selectively blind themselves in order not to see this painful and perilous set of circumstances. A student described what happened when his thesis advisor used him as a spy:

> My department decided to make a permanent full-time position out of the part-time position held by my thesis advisor. She very badly wanted the job and strongly suggested I be one of the students on the search committee. I thought it would help my standing among the other faculty members so I volunteered. These committees are confidential; nothing is supposed to be told to anyone on the outside.
>
> In the course of the search, it did not go well for my teacher. When we selected our top candidates, the chairperson asked each of us to talk about who was acceptable and who was not. My advisor was basically voted an unacceptable candidate by everyone.
>
> Even though my advisor was told she hadn't been selected, she wanted to know everything that had happened and began to drill me. She's very persistent and can pump like mad. She's very, very hard to turn off. I felt guilty for not supporting her on the committee and I was scared to stand up to her. She seemed so upset and was building it all out of proportion.
>
> To calm her down, I told her in a general way what had happened. She took what I said and went to another committee member to get more information. Then she came back to me and asked if what she had heard was true. She turned what she learned from me into a huge case and eventually threatened to sue the department for not having offered the job to her.
>
> I felt awful. I was a traitor for not voting for her and a traitor to the committee. I felt responsible for her welfare and responsible for the mess that happened.

In this example, the student was at risk regardless of what position he took. If he broke confidentiality and gave his advisor the information, he would break the trust of the committee. If he refused his advisor, she would see him as a traitor to her cause. Since she held the greater power in the relationship and made him feel responsible for her feelings, he responded to her pressure and violated his own standards.

Having betrayed his own principles, he was thrown into an even deeper personal bind as he joined the duplicity by allowing her to get away with using him and others to get confidential information illegitimately. If he confronted her about her manipulation of him, he would risk her revealing his part in breaking confidentiality. This possibility could jeopardize his credibility in the department. If he did nothing, however, he would feel like a guilty co-conspirator and she could continue to use him as her agent.

The Indulgence of Personal Privilege

In every boundary violation, there is a fit between the professional's need and the client's vulnerability. This coupling produces the opportunity for the professional to take advantage of the client. Indeed, since the professional has the authority over and the responsibility for the client's situation, he or she is particularly susceptible to extending the privilege of his or her superior position and intruding on the client. The professional's decision to act on this opportunity grows out his or her presumption that he or she can use his or her privilege to do whatever he or she wants with the client.

Once the professional substitutes his or her agenda for the ethos of care, his or her energy is directed toward an illegitimate goal. He or she operates out of a different place internally. The professional justifies his or her control with the belief that the client's situation belongs to him or her rather than is being entrusted to his or her care temporarily. The motive of the professional stems from his or her own self-gratification rather than from a sense of obligation to the client. The intrusiveness of the professional on the client grows out of a sense of entitlement rather than a mutually established relationship. These fundamental changes in position reflect the professional's switch from helping the client to gratifying himself or herself by controlling the client's life. A client described how her minister exploited their relationship and presumed to take from her for his own purposes:

> I was having major sexual and financial problems with my husband and was worried about the delinquent behavior of my children. I had been to see my minister several times for his advice. I remember I always felt scared when he gave his sermons. He always started by saying, "A woman walked into my office. She was such and such an age and she had these problems." I always feel this pit in my stomach and thought that maybe he was going to talk about me. He never began his sermons with stories about men. The details that he shared about these women didn't even seem related to the main point of his talk.
>
> Anyway, I remember one Sunday he began talking about this woman who was my age and described the specific sexual and financial concerns she had with her husband. I felt really embarrassed but also really special because he had chosen a story about me for his sermon. I remember sitting with my friend and having her say to me, "You know, that sounds like you." That's when I really started to feel unsafe. It started to feel real messy because he had so much personal information about me.

In this example, the minister capitalized on the relationship and used the parishioner for his own purposes. He extended the privilege of his position: He believed he had the right to use her personal material, which was given in a private counseling session, as his subject matter in a public sermon. Rather than registering that it was incumbent on him to get her permission, he circumvented the relationship and gave himself the permission to violate her confidence. In doing so, he controlled her freedom to determine how her personal information would be used.

As shown in this example, the indulgence of personal privilege is propelled by the immediacy of the professional's need and by his or her motive in the relationship. Since the purpose of the professional-client relationship is to serve the client, however, professionals who extend their privilege have to establish a legitimate claim to intrude and some reason to explain behavior that is otherwise incongruent with the ethos of care. They have to persuade themselves that their behavior is either inconsequential or helpful and necessary for the client. In effect, they must hide their true impulses.

As a result, these professionals couch their motives in language that justifies their actions, the most frequent rationalization being that their behavior is "for the client." A therapist who was given expensive computer software by a client explained her behavior and why she kept the gifts:

> I wanted to get this client who was a computer salesman to talk to me so I moved into a social discussion with him. Since he was having so much trouble dealing with all his problems and didn't trust me, I made him more comfortable by talking about my problems with computers. I asked him to teach me how to program different things. He began making copies of programs and sending them to me in the mail. I did not refuse them because I wanted them, I couldn't get them, and I saved myself a lot of money. What was most important, though, was that I couldn't give them back because then he would feel rejected.

In this example, the professional explained away her self-serving behavior first by convincing herself that she had to make her client comfortable by reframing their therapeutic relationship as a reciprocal friendship and later by deciding that she could not return the gifts because she might hurt him.

Redefining responsibility as "I had to," reframing care as "I know what is best for you," or interpreting neglectful or abusive behavior as justified by some lofty objective or important principle of human concern camouflages the professional's intent. The claim of benevolence allows the professional to hide his or her true motives behind a veil of reasonableness. A client who was sexually abused by her minister described the twisted logic he used to explain how his staying with his wife would be "best for her":

> This minister told me that he would never leave his wife and marry me because I would want to have children. He had had a vasectomy. He told me that if I loved him that much, I would want to have his child. Since he couldn't give me his child, we would never live happily ever after. Therefore, he would take care of my problem by never leaving his wife. His doing that became a favor to me because he knew I would be miserable because I couldn't have his baby.

Another client described how her physician justified changing her mind about her care because she was "doing it for the client":

> I was the receptionist for this physician. I was also her patient. I was pregnant and began to have premature labor at 30 weeks. She knew I needed bed rest and should be home and off my feet. I didn't know it at the time but the business manager disagreed. He was concerned about my being off work but getting paid some ridiculously small amount of money in benefits. He evidently told the doctor that either I would have to work or they would have to terminate my employment. I had been a dedicated employee for two years and had never missed a day of work.
>
> My doctor changed her medical decision and said, "You're not that far dilated. Your cervix is just a little soft. I think you can work four hours a day and you'll be fine." She believed she was helping me and protecting my job by letting me work. Yet, she made the decision for me and justified it as medically based.

All of these examples illustrate the professional's issues with control and ownership that occur in boundary violations. Since the professional's job is to take charge of what the client needs, taking control can seem a legitimate part of the professional's role and appear natural to the client. Since defining the reality of the situation is also part of the professional's role, justifying the indulgence of personal privilege as professionally warranted by the client's condition or situation again appears congruent with what the client expects. Using the official script to hide the truth effectively blocks and distorts the client's perceptions. The client's opportunity to see or to question may be delayed for a long time.

THE PROCESS OF A BOUNDARY VIOLATION

As already stated, the reversal of roles, one or more secrets, a double bind and the indulgence of personal privilege are the characteristics of a boundary violation. The indulgence of personal privilege allows the professional to pursue the relationship for his or her own purposes. This misdirection of power spans the boundary violation. The spin-off from this is the creation of the secret of a dual agenda. Since the professional's needs now structure the inside of the relationship, the professional and the client reverse roles. Not realizing what has happened, the client is confronted with two conflicting realities that double bind and block him or her from leaving the relationship. While the secret, reversal of roles, and double bind are created and fueled by the professional's initial move, they also become the structural props that support the altered system between the professional and the client and allow it to flourish. The synergy among all four characteristics provides the new system with a life force of its own.

A boundary violation requires the interlocking presence of all four characteristics. Together, they spawn a series of relational changes that damage the professional-client bond. The collective impact of these changes erodes the boundaries that allow a safe connection for both the professional and the client. In the following story, a client describes how her therapist misused his power to turn her therapy into a long-term proposition. While direct sexual contact never occurred, the client had to wrestle with the volatility of her feelings because of his constant seduction. Her story typifies the process of a boundary violation.

I consulted a counselor about my disintegrating marriage. Having described how impossible my husband was, I added a comment at the end of the session about how I knew that I, too, wasn't perfect. As I got up to leave, the counselor patted me reassuringly on the back and said, "But you're still a valuable person." That felt so good. I hadn't heard that in a long time. He was so validating. After I had seen him a few more times, he asked how I felt about him. I said I was developing a silly crush on him. I felt embarrassed to talk about it, but since he was a therapist, I assumed I could be honest.

The secret of her therapist's interest in her emerges in the next two suggestive interchanges.

(1) He asked me why I thought the crush was silly. I answered, "Because I'm married and you're married." He retorted, "You're wrong. I'm not married, but you are and that's enough for me." It wasn't the fact that he was my therapist that kept him from going to bed with me. It was the fact that I was married. (2) Much of the time, he sat next to me on the couch. During one session, I told him I really liked him. He reached over and kind of touched my back and rubbed my neck a little and said, "That's good, because I like you too."

This was probably the first time in my life that I met someone whom I respected and liked and who liked me back in a way I thought was personal. I got obsessional about how I looked for him. Everything had to be perfect right down to my lipstick and nails. I had never felt so good in my whole life. When I talked to him on the phone, I'd have so much energy for the next three hours that I could get my whole apartment cleaned and the wash done and everything else.

The reversal of roles surfaces as the client describes her awareness of her therapist's neediness.

It's funny. The first couple of times I saw him I thought he was a nerd. It was just a quick impression. But when he began to fill all my needs, he became something wonderful. It was almost a relief when I stopped seeing him and I could go to therapy looking scruffy if I felt like it.

The secret of the therapist's seduction becomes more obvious as the client describes the range of invitations he continued to offer. All of them double bind her.

One time I brought a paper about my philosophy of life for him to read. I had written it as part of a school assignment and I thought it might help him understand me. After reading the paper, he asked me, "How come you didn't put in there that you're sexy?" Another time he asked me if I wanted a hug. I like to hug people, so I said, "Yes, that's fine." Maybe he meant his hugs to be just friendly, but they were turning me on a lot and he would comment on my passion.

The client comments on the reversal of roles and her therapist's continuous encouragement of her participation.

I was very upfront with my feelings. I remember I said to him, "These feelings I have for you are tearing me apart because I care so much for you and when I walk out of here you probably don't think of me until you see me at the next session." Right there he should have stopped it and said, "You need to talk about this." Instead, he continued to foster my feelings. He corrected me,

"How do you know what I feel? How can you know or assume to know what I feel?" I felt weird about what was happening, so I asked him if this happened with his other women clients. He told me that it had happened with a few but reassured me that none had responded as fully as I had.

The reversal of roles becomes more overt.

My therapist had apparently received some bad news and looked sad as he sat in one corner of the couch. He asked me, "Do you think sometimes you could just love me?" I reassured him that I knew I did without any doubts. Then he asked, "How come I seem to be able to form a long-lasting friendship or relationship with my clients or they seem to be able to love me and I can't seem to do this outside the sessions?" I can't believe I said this, but I answered him by saying, "You know, it's sort of easy to maintain a relationship one hour every two weeks." Who the hell was the therapist here anyway!

The counselor introduces another secret and forms a tighter alliance by sharing his history. The client's empathic response illustrates the reversal of roles that automatically follows the creation of a dual agenda.

Whenever he shared information about himself, I felt compelled to give to him. His invitation to me to respond to him was frequently disguised in self-disclosing comments. One time, I shared with him that I had been sexually abused by two 16-year-old boys when I was 11. He sat and listened to me and then asked, "Was your blouse open?" Then he told me about a sexual abuse incident that happened to him as a young boy. It was like we shared this together. When he told me about what happened to him, I almost fell into the role of feeling sorry for him and thinking I should take care of him. I didn't think what he did was inappropriate because I saw him as a counselor with credentials after his name. Now I know a friendship was developing.

The reversal of roles continues.

Following one of our sessions, we went for a walk after a fresh snowfall. It was very pretty, very romantic out. He started talking to me about his sister and what she would do when it started to snow heavily. I shut him off right in the middle of his conversation and started talking about myself at work. I went home that night feeling so guilty because I hadn't let him keep talking.

The termination of the therapy merely reinforces the secret of their real but unofficial relationship.

He told me we would have to terminate if there was ever to be more. So I terminated therapy with him at his office and then we went and had supper. While we were hugging, I said, "I'm not such a bad person. I would be really good in a relationship." He replied, "Yes, you would but probably not with your husband." I asked, "What about you?" He said, "We'll see."

There was never a clear ending. Even though he was in charge, he instructed me that I was to make the future contact when he said "Well, I can't call you, but you can call me." I left feeling really high and thinking that this was great. Yet, another time when we had supper, he changed his mind and said, "I can't see you any-more. They would hang me up by my toenails if I did." I was totally confused when he called a week later and said, "Since we've spent a lot of time together, I called to find out if you were okay."

The client attempts to resolve the double bind both by ending the relationship and by releasing herself from the feelings that held her prisoner. Her moves are thwarted when she asks her therapist to take some responsibility.

After I started with a new therapist, I asked my previous coun-selor to meet me for lunch. I told him that clients frequently fall in love with their therapists but it's dealt with in the office. I said, "What I want to hear from you is that you never want to see me again. I want to know that all those things you said to me were a crock of bull. Then maybe I can get on with my life and maybe get you out of my system." He responded, "Well, I can never say that to anybody."

The client expresses her double bind.

I felt helpless and at fault because I couldn't stop caring about him. It's hard to give up something that makes you feel good. Yet, I don't want to admit to myself that I was so stupid. I can't believe that two people who have a lot in common and seem to really care for each other don't really matter to each other. It's hard to believe that someone can say all those things and be that close to you, but in his mind it's all in the name of therapy. I felt like he was the best person I'd ever met. I don't know that I could care that much again for anyone. I would have given up anything, almost anything.

The four characteristics of a boundary violation enumerated earlier surface repeatedly throughout the story. The reversal in role occurs when the therapist's structures the inside of the relationship according to his needs. First, he unilaterally shifted the client's status and made her feel special. She, in turn, attended to the therapist's apparently poor sexual self-image by letting him know in a variety of ways that she found him attractive. While consciously she believed he was doing it for her, the reality of whose needs were primary became evident when she said, "It was almost a relief when I stopped seeing him and I could go to therapy looking scruffy if I felt like it."

She attended to him whenever they discussed his relationship problems. Assigned responsibility for his feelings as a man, she answered his question and reassured him she loved him without any doubts. Even though she was an unequal participant, she became his therapist when she said, "You know, it's sort of easy to maintain a relationship one hour

every two weeks." When they discussed her sexual abuse, he moved in
with his own. Responding to the stirrings of empathy for him, she said,
"I almost fell into the role of feeling sorry for him and thinking I should
have taken care of him." When he talked about his sister, she refused to
attend directly to his needs but admitted, "I went home that night feeling
guilty because I didn't let him keep talking." Since all of these incidents
took place under the aegis of therapy, the pretense of normalcy fostered
the client's exploitation and encouraged her to participate as part of her
treatment.

The primary secret in this vignette is the fantasized but nonphysical
sexual affair. Since the therapist was seducing the client while pretending
she is in therapy, he was able to gain her cooperation without fully
disclosing his agenda. In retrospect, however, the seeds of the violation
were sown in the beginning but immediately normalized and disregarded. The therapist's comment that the client was a valuable person
initially passed for validation of her self-worth. Seen within the total
context of his hidden agenda, however, its meaning changes, becoming
part of his persistent exercise in seductive flattery.

The therapist acted out of the secret when he sat beside her on the
couch and rubbed her neck and back. They embraced and he com-
mented on her passion. Rather than being available as a therapist, he
played hard to get. Feeling alone in the relationship, the client bemoaned
the torment of her infatuation. They took nighttime walks together and
shared dinner after her supposed counseling sessions. Because of the dual
agenda, she had difficulty discerning what was real. Indeed, she considered his behaviors a part of her therapy for which she literally paid him a
fee. Since he was the therapist and defined reality, she was not free to
trust her perceptions.

The other major secret in this boundary violation is the joining of the
therapist and the client against the husband who was on the outside and
did not know about the affair. Even though the client originally sought
therapy because of her disintegrating marriage, the triangle of deceit

formed by the therapist directly undermined any chance for it. As he became the favored suitor, the unknowing husband was victimized.

The double binding of this client was especially toxic. She was blind to the emotional blackmail that controlled her actions. To keep feeling good about herself as a woman, she had to keep making the therapist feel good about himself as a man. Her perceived value arose from what she must give the therapist to keep getting from him what she wanted and needed. Without him, she felt she was nothing. To stay in this relationship made her sick; to leave thrust her into despair. Either way she lost.

Throughout the therapy, the therapist indulged his personal privilege by placing his wants ahead of the client's needs. Entitled, he intruded on her marriage by building a sexualized relationship with her, intruded on her body by rubbing her neck and back, intruded on her therapy with his own history of sexual abuse, and intruded on her privacy by questioning her feelings for him. Operating from within himself rather than from inside the therapeutic relationship, he took permission to extend his privilege with no regard for his impact on the client. Indeed, when the client told him she was scared and out of control, he reprimanded her for assuming his feelings were not mutual: "Right there he should have stopped it and said, 'You need to talk about this.' Instead, he continued to foster my feelings. He corrected me, 'How do you know what I feel?'" All the while knowing he had entered forbidden waters— "They could hang me up by my toenails"—he continued to use her to feel adequate as a man by encouraging the continuation of the relationship. He camouflaged the truth, however, by eliciting her sexual responsiveness so that she, not he, looked needy and dependent. Therefore, he justified what he did by rationalizing that it was only in response to her needs. His assumed benevolence was a critical ingredient in the emotional sabotage of the client's therapy.

In this story, the four characteristics combine to support the system between the therapist and the client. The therapist's indulgence of personal privilege allowed him to alter the ethos of care and place his own needs first. Acting out of the secret, he responded to the client seductively and enticed her to feel special by responding to his needs. Each time she complied with his direction, she supported the secret by participating in the reversal of roles. As she went deeper into the relationship, she grew more double bound and dependent on feeling special. Since she was less free to move within the relationship based on her own therapeutic needs, the therapist exploited her low self-worth by making her hungry for his attention. To keep the system going, she had to continue ◆ to feed him by her response to his suggestions, which, in turn, furthered his agenda and reinforced his assumption of privilege. The circular movement among these elements gave this boundary violation its momentum. The distortion of the relationship infected the legitimate system of care, confusing and harming the client.

CONSEQUENCES TO THE RELATIONSHIP

Many boundary violations go unrecognized. Unknowing clients may never realize that a physician financially benefited from an unnecessary medical procedure or that an attorney risked an unlikely defense in order to establish his or her reputation. Boundary violations may also begin as innocent situations that feel good to professional and client alike. When both are unaware of the danger and potential harm, a parishioner's offer to serve as financial advisor to the minister, a client's invitation to become friends with the therapist, or a teacher's caring and gentle interest in the sexual preference of a student are experienced as attractive opportunities to expand the relationship. Given the context of the offer or the expectation of compliance that marks the professional relationship, questioning the intent of the initiator may seem inappropriate. Therefore, many violations progress to dangerous places before they are recognized. Indeed, the violations are usually not felt until something goes wrong, and the client has reason to question the arrangement. As the consequences emerge, the client begins to experience the pain and the damage generated by the professional's failure to protect the covenant.

● Clients resist seeing this truth. Orphaned by us professionals, they are still in need. To recognize the wound to their spirit would place in jeopardy their willingness to trust other professionals. Therefore, they protect their faith by continuing to believe that our actions were based on our concern for their well-being. Caught between their need to trust and the danger that can result, they distort reality and maintain their loyalty to us in order to resist the ensuing depression and despair.

The wound to the relationship, however, is also a wound to the understanding that forms the covenant of faith between us professionals and society. Since we are both our clients' caretakers and servants of society, and since our clients give us their trust out of that larger framework, our betrayal of the mutual commitment betrays the fundamental promise of allegiance between us and society. The ramifications are significant. Not knowing whom to trust or what to believe, clients increasingly sense the erosion of the spiritual base between us. By destroying the spirit of our mutual endeavor, boundary violations gradually and subtly weaken the fiber of the professional-client connection.

The misbehavior of any one of us causes clients to mistrust others of us who are in the same profession. Consequently, we too are indirectly affected by the behavior of our colleagues. The rise in legal actions of professional misconduct, the reduction in standards of care, and the ascendancy of profit as the yardstick of professional success suggest that our obligation to clients is increasingly compromised by other interests. Indeed, each unaddressed boundary violation helps create the cynicism that characterizes the attitudes of many clients today.

As professionals, we do not usually think in such broad terms. Many violations are small and seemingly insignificant when they are not upfront and apparent. No one of us believes our individual actions could produce such wide-ranging results. Since only our clients directly experience the violation, it is hard for us professionals to understand the magnitude of the consequences that echo through our clients' lives. Listening to their stories can help us to learn more. Learning to recognize the four characteristics of a boundary violation begins to make more understandable the damage reported by clients. These same elements also become the beacons by which we can examine the health of the relationship.

V

PSYCHOLOGICAL WOUNDS: THE VICTIM'S RESPONSE

B OUNDARY VIOLATIONS ARE relational wounds in that the trust between professional and client is damaged. While each violation has
its own unique circumstances, the common experience of victimized
clients is that of a double-cross. The covenant that should unite the
professional and the client turns out to be a falsehood. Rather than being
a recipient of the professional's allegiance and commitment, the client is
victimized by the professional's disloyalty and self-interest.

While the violation is to the covenant between the professional and
the client, the harmful consequences land solely on the client. Some of
the manifestations are external. A student may delay or scuttle his career
plans because of a professor's inappropriate behavior. A client may feel
the need to hire a new attorney because the former one breached
confidentiality by sharing information about another client. A client
may need hospitalization because a therapist's failure to recognize
boundaries jeopardized her emotional stability. A patient may avoid

seeking any future medical attention as a result of his physician's misbehavior.

Other manifestations are internal. A client may castigate himself for being a wimp because he could not stop his therapist from emotionally abusing him. A patient may feel terror and be continuously on guard with other physicians once she realizes her trusted family physician manipulated her physical responses during an examination. A client may feel ashamed because he initially enjoyed and responded to the extra attention he received from his rabbi who later exploited their connection.

These consequences shake clients' internal foundations. Trying to find a cause-and-effect explanation for the violation, they ask, "Why did this happen?" "What did I do?" "Why didn't I see it coming?" Since the violation strikes at the core of the beliefs that clients use to navigate in the world, they feel disoriented and disillusioned. Trying to get their grounding, they ask, "Who can you trust?" "How do you know when you are safe?" Unless the professional is available to help them sort out these questions, clients are set adrift and frequently become preoccupied by all that remains unanswered.

Without the professional's involvement, clients are abandoned twice, first because the professional violated them and second because he or she left them to manage the pain alone. If the professional fails to take responsibility for the injury, clients are left to struggle with the ambiguity inherent in the violation. Lacking the clarity that only the professional can give, their perceptions of what really happened are obscured. What they need to do remains unclear.

If the professional does not acknowledge and explain his or her part, clients, in the midst of their isolation, are apt to take on the whole of it. They may shoulder the blame, condemning themselves for their involvement.

If the professional does not repair the breach of trust, clients may be wary and feel they are left with no other remedy than to avoid any situation that might replay their hurtful experience with the professional.

If the professional does not validate clients' realities, clients may turn to outsiders who do not understand. Confidants may blame the client; deny, minimize, or normalize the violation; or ask the client to excuse the professional's behavior. The danger to clients escalates as they turn against themselves and internalize the wound to the relationship. Moreover, their struggle to cope with the pain leaves them wholly responsible for handling what really belongs to the professional.

EXTERNAL VERSUS INTERNAL DAMAGE ASSESSMENT

Every boundary violation damages the professional-client relationship. However, infractions vary in severity as defined externally by law, professional regulations, customs, and societal mores. Sexual abuse, mismanagement of funds, and gross medical neglect resulting in misdiagnosis or physical injury are some practices that are clearly recognized as egregious. Socializing or forming friendships with clients, asking students for personal favors, and engaging clients in business endeavors raise less concern. Determining severity by content alone does not allow a violation to be identified as legitimate or valid unless and until it has progressed to the most severe and overt extreme. Indeed, those violations that do not fit within particular categories are ignored or seen as not serious.

To get a truer, more comprehensive picture, it is essential that degree of pain felt by clients be measured. When a reading of their internal experience is taken, the impact varies according to the context of the relationship, each client's particular makeup, and the meaning each client assigns to the transgression. Indeed, for one client, a violation may cause a severe emotional reaction; for another, the same violation may cause only mild discomfort. A professional's invitation to lunch, therefore, may be absorbed as a non-event by one client but be interpreted by another as having important personal ramifications. Instead of using an external measure that extracts the violation from its context and alters its meaning, assessing the damage according to the internal experience of clients gives a more valid picture and makes the violation legitimate because of its impact.

Initial Responses to Abandonment: Shock, Shame, and Denial

The break in the connection leaves clients stranded. Jolted by the professional's disloyalty, clients first react with disbelief. When they begin to grasp what has happened, some clients shrug their shoulders and move on. They adapt by shrinking the professional down to size. For them, the issue is closed but not resolved. Other clients are so scared and stunned that they dissociate from their feelings to keep from being emotionally overwhelmed and begin to respond mechanically out of their numbness. A client described her sense of abandonment, her fear for her future treatment, her feeling of being exploited, and the vigilant posture she maintained in response to her therapist's desertion of the relationship:

> The organization I worked for was interviewing three candidates as possible consultants. One of the candidates was my therapist's business partner. My therapist knew that I was a part of the group making the decision. I remember sharing my concerns with her and asking, "How's this going to be? She's your partner and I don't want you talking about what I'm doing in therapy with her." She assured me that she would maintain confidentiality.
>
> At our next session, however, she said to me, "I hope my partner gets the job because she really wants it." I was mad. I think I felt sort of used. Yet, I also felt desperate. I figured that if I didn't go along with what she wanted, she might leave me. It felt like a betrayal. She was talking about something she wanted for a col-

league, while I was saying that I didn't think this would be good
for me in terms of my therapy. Since she had dropped her role, it
put me more on guard and I was extra watchful of the process.

Clients feel diminished when their primary needs are moved to a
lesser position. Having assumed that they were safe, that their needs
came first, and that the professional cared about them, clients feel
devalued as persons deserving respect when they are victimized. Some
react with anger. Many feel humiliated and keep the violation a secret.
Still others do not feel much because the let-down is familiar and
matches their low self-esteem. Since the shame that creeps in under-
mines their confidence, clients frequently find themselves questioning
their rights. A client who was verbally abused by a therapist described
his shame and the impact of the violation on his ability to claim what he
needed for himself:

> My therapist encouraged me to share some of my feelings in a
> group. When I finished, he asked me if I was always that weird.
> Since I was teased for being sensitive in my family, the last thing I
> wanted was to appear weird. His saying that pushed me back
> down all the more. I didn't know what to say in response.
> I felt I got mocked for expressing my feelings. It confirmed for
> me that you don't share those things. If you do, someone will call
> you strange. I was frightened to talk to anyone. Instead I berated
> myself for having had such a strong response. To acknowledge or
> admit that what had happened was traumatic and terrifying would
> mean that I was fragile and couldn't handle this thing.

Not knowing what to do, clients commonly handle the stress by
emotionally distancing themselves from the situation. They may ignore,
deny, minimize, or rationalize the professional's behavior. A client
shared what happened when a therapist invited her husband to play
chess:

At the end of our first marital counseling session, the counselor discovered my husband was a chess player and suggested they get together to play. Since we had all agreed that the marriage was hopeless, the counselor thought therapy was finished. At the time, the counselor's behavior didn't affect me because the marriage was over and I wanted to be rid of my husband. It detracted from my respect for the counselor, however, and I decided he was a turkey. I was lucky it didn't do any damage. At another time in my life it could have been devastating. Today, though, I think it's funny and I'm amused by the fact that these two turkeys have been playing chess for nearly twenty years.

This same client later admitted that this situation was more painful than she had realized. "I'm close to tears," she said. "These things really do affect people. I'm an example of someone who acts as if it doesn't matter."

For a time, denial allows clients to psychologically control the size and impact of the violation. Decreasing its magnitude reduces the incongruence between the professional's self-serving behavior and his or her moral and legal obligation to the client. Decreasing its significance makes it less potent and therefore less painful. By telling themselves that the violation did not happen, that it happened but it had no harmful consequences, that it happened but I was to blame, or that it happened but it was no big deal, clients feel more in charge and less vulnerable. Unfortunately, they regain their footing at the cost of discounting their reality.

Although many victimized clients go on with their lives without significant pain, they always carry a residue of loss, disillusionment, and disappointment. Although they regain their equilibrium, their losses are forever etched in their memories—loss of control over what happened to them, loss of safety in the relationship, loss of trust in the professional, loss of confidence in terms of their ability to watch out for themselves, and loss of self-esteem at having been deserted by the professional. These feelings to a greater or lesser extent never dissipate if the professional fails to address what happened in the relationship and attend to the client's sense of injury. Crouched low inside themselves, clients monitor their safety and replace their trust with watchful caution.

Internalization of the Violation

Depending upon the size of the violation and the relational context, many clients are constantly confronted by the pain and aftermath of the violation. Unable to get away from what has happened or is happening, clients begin to carry what the professional did in the relationship within themselves.

Once internalized, the violation exists separate from any rational process aimed at directing the client's behavior. Now the dialogue is within the client rather than between the client and the professional. Indeed, the client develops an independent relationship with the violation. A client described how she internalized the violation after she was initially elevated as special and later abused by her minister:

> When I was in the eighth grade, my father came down with leukemia. He was ashamed of being ill and never talked about it. Because of his no-talk rule, I couldn't tell anyone. That was awful for me because it turned it into a shameful secret.
>
> I felt connected to the youth minister. After a long time, I was able to tell him that my dad was sick and that I was scared to death and very lonely. For four years, he counseled me. I loved and adored him and gave him presents. He treated me like an adult and I always felt very special. My father died when I was 18 and this minister buried him.
>
> Shortly thereafter, he began to be sexual. He would hug, kiss, and caress me. I remember him saying, "I can't imagine why you would want to stay a virgin." He was planting seeds. I began wondering if something was wrong with me. He eventually asked me to spend the night with him. I told him I would if he promised

not to touch me. We went to bed and he was all over me. I was afraid and told him I had to go to the bathroom. I was so scared and nervous that I could not urinate. When I thought he was sleeping, I climbed back into bed. He was wide-awake though and kept pressuring me until I relented and gave in.

In time, I stopped seeing him. But then I started having all these problems. I would have anger fits in which I would just be outraged. I became suicidal and started cutting myself a lot. I starved myself and exercised to an extreme. I just didn't have a lot of concern for how my body felt. I had learned that I wasn't important and my body wasn't important. I ended up in a psych ward.

I still struggle with wanting closeness and wanting to be the most favorite. One of the ways you can do that is to be sexual with the people to whom you want to be special. This action means you're really special. I think I needed to believe that so that I didn't have to look at how I had been taken advantage of.

I still get being violated, having sex, and being emotionally close all mixed up. My husband and I have a nice, safe relationship—and I don't want to wreck it with sex. It's a control thing for me. I don't believe any of this would have happened if this minister had not entered my life. I'm still real inhibited sexually, and it all goes right back to him.

This client internalized the violation, making herself suffer for the hurt caused by her minister. She treated herself like the object she was to him and reexperienced the psychological damage whenever she felt confused about her sexuality and what made her special.

MISDIRECTED ATTEMPTS TO MASTER THE PAIN

Clients go to extraordinary lengths to manage the pain of the internalized violation. Since they find it intolerable to experience simultaneously the painful truth of their losses, their vulnerability, and their aloneness in a situation where they believed they were being watched over, they make valiant efforts to protect themselves from being emotionally overwhelmed. They try to clarify what happened so that they feel less anxious and confused. They try to make themselves safe so that they feel less frightened. They try to take complete responsibility so that they feel less helpless. They seek validation so that they feel less alone.

For many clients, these attempts to master the pain are in vain. They run into obstacles that block the success of their efforts. Moreover, the measures they take often result in great cost to themselves.

Blocks to Gaining Clarity

The obsessional thinking of clients reflects their efforts to sort through the debris around them to find clarity. They work their head hard to fathom what happened or is happening and thus get on top of the situation. Believing that comprehension will provide a sense of mastery, they search for a story line about what went wrong and why. They seek a logic that will bring order to what otherwise seems a capricious and unpredictable sequence of events.

Lacking information from the professional, clients try to fill in the missing pieces on their own. Often, they draw on their own belief systems, which may or may not be accurate. For example, a patient might decide that a physician was offensive in his conversation because he was confused about how to lessen her anxiety. Another patient might decide that he was angry because she was bothering him with her questions. Still another patient might feel that he was brusque because he had previously had an angry interchange with her husband.

Clients frequently introduce explanations that are congruent with their self-image and life experiences. Although their explanations may be distorted or even delusional, clients have no other option but to fall back on that which is familiar. Unfortunately, because their vision is obstructed by the professional, a lack of information, or erroneous explanations, they are barred from the clarity they so need. A student described the meaning she made out of a teacher's behavior:

> From the beginning, I felt like she wanted to tell me things about her. She was real transparent and her insecurity was apparent. She wanted me to like her or approve of her. One time she told me her family had come to town for her brother's wedding. As she told me, she sunk back in her chair. I immediately interpreted that she was having some discomfort with not being married herself. I didn't want her to feel bad. I wanted to tell her how special she was and to take care of her in some way.

Two Realities

With a boundary violation comes two realities. The first and official relationship between professional and client already exists. It establishes the formal and legitimate reality built around the client's need. A boundary violation, however, twists the relationship and establishes a second and duplicitous reality, one that is covertly built around the professional's needs. Clients' inability to gain clarity stems from living with these two realities. They are left swimming in a murky pool of ambiguity. Indeed, the spawning of the second, conflicting reality is one of the worst consequences of boundary violations, because clients are held captive in a confused state where they cannot decide what is real and what they should believe.

The covert reality arises from a reversal of roles and a mixed agenda. The victim of a boundary violation is already a client of the professional. However, when the professional uses the client to fulfill his or her needs, the client is forced into the role of caretaker. This lowers the client's status, which adversely affects his or her identity and feelings of self-worth. If, for example, the client is given special treatment, he or she may initially feel powerful. Unfortunately, as the client becomes aware of what has happened, he or she may also feel diminished. Caught in the middle of a paradox, the client cannot assess reality, his or her relative power, and who he or she is in the relationship. An art student who was courted and harassed by her professor expressed her confusion about having received a scholarship: "I'll never know if I was chosen because of my talent or because this teacher wanted to score with me."

While the official agenda, or intent, of the relationship is to take care of the client's needs, another agenda emerges when the professional uses the relationship to fulfill his or her own needs. The professional's intent is often disguised, however, under a cloak of concern for the client. Understandably, the client is baffled as to the professional's true agenda and bewildered by the professional's deceit. A client described her confusion when a physician began asking questions about and making references to her sex life:

> I went to this doctor because I had the flu. He asked me personal things about my dating. He told me that he thought I was depressed and needed to have a social life and get laid. Every time I went to see him, he asked me these questions. If it had happened only once, I would have thought he was joking, but it kept happening and I started to put some importance on it. I envied him because he seemed to have a carefree attitude about sex. Part of me didn't take him seriously, but another part of me did. I wanted to know more about him and why he was making these comments. I wanted to know if I was making this stuff up or if there was some truth to it.

Even as clients become aware of the second agenda imposed by the professional, they are handicapped in their search for clarification by the fact that they cannot tell which agenda is primary. Since both are going on simultaneously and are interwoven with each other, clients cannot accurately sort out the implications of the situation or the meaning of events. They cannot figure out how to respond. They can only speculate about the professional's motive and frequently have to base their conclusions on inference.

Confusion in Decision-Making

Faced with two realities, clients cannot see safe options about how they should proceed. Since the truth eludes them, they feel unsure about what they are seeing and experiencing. They therefore have no solid foundation from which to make their decisions. Indeed, they find that each solution jeopardizes something else they value. A client who was uncertain about whether or not her attorney was being seductive expressed it this way:

> Maybe I am doing something to lead him on, but if I change the rules and become more rigid, he may take it as rejection and not work as hard on my case. If I say something to him, he may be insulted. If I do nothing, it may get worse. I don't even know if my perceptions are accurate.

In their decision-making, clients also struggle with the unfairness of having to pay an additional price to protect themselves from the person or the institution entrusted to be their caretaker. A seminary student described the cost to herself and her career as she struggled with the realization that members of the church hierarchy had set her up as being competent, select, and special while hiding their true intentions and expectations that she be submissive to their will in the future:

> While I was a student, I was used by the church. Since there aren't many women in the church, I was targeted and a token at the same time. Before I could be ordained as a elder, some clerics were supposed to interview me to determine whether or not I was ready, but they began visiting with me instead. I had written thirty to forty pages of material for this event. They said, "We want you to know that we have already made up our minds, so let's just get rid of the anxiety you are feeling and talk as colleagues." At first, I took it as a compliment, inferring that I was so superior in my work in the church that they didn't want me to be anxious. As time went on, all that changed. They began asking me how I had

raised so much money for the church at which I was a student minister. Some of them wanted me to come to their churches. All of a sudden, I was the expert.

As I was driving away, I realized that I hadn't been treated the same as the rest of my peers. It was a kind of reverse discrimination. All of the papers I had written for this interview were not valued equally like everyone else's. I had taken this interview seriously and was being very open. I was hoping for their feedback and I didn't get that. Although I was placed on this little pedestal, I was still dismissed. Even the district superintendent said, "We are really keeping our eye on you because we are expecting great things from you." Initially it was a tribute, but later I felt a lot of pressure.

Gradually I realized that the church hierarchy didn't care about my needs as a person and that they were mainly concerned for themselves. I was trapped in a system that was killing my integrity because people said one thing and did another. At the same time, the church rewards those who jump through the hoops.

I stopped caring about myself until I made the decision to leave the church. I lost weight and was borderline anemic. I lost the urge to write in my journal and I lost the ability to cry. It took me a long time to figure this out. Because my ordination was a year and a half away, I had to keep going.

I'm just now seeing how much I was an object and that realization is sometimes staggering. There have been lots of tears trying to get myself back. I still have a difficult time setting foot in a church. Nowadays, I struggle to pay my bills, but I feel more authentic. I have taken a job as chaplain for a hospital, which means my health insurance and pension benefits were cut, my salary was cut in half, and I lost the housing provided by the church.

Dual roles and mixed agendas keep the boundary of the relationship ill-defined. The resulting confusion keeps clients paralyzed. Being held in a state of limbo magnifies their vulnerability. A client compared her difficulty in seeing reality with having an eye examination: "When the optometrist tries out different lenses and rotates them for clarity, I always feel sick to my stomach. There's that point when I have double or even triple vision for a second before the lines come together."

Because the coexistence of two realities distorts and filters what they can see, clients mentally reenact their history with the professional in an attempt to explain away their confusion. Without a perceptual map that allows synthesis of discrepant facts, however, clients cannot assess their power in the relationship, the meaning of the professional's behavior, or their priorities and possible options. Their lack of success compels them to search even harder. Rather than finding a way out, they are often bound tighter to an endless and unrewarding pursuit.

Blocks to Gaining Safety

Safety precedes all other human needs except physical survival (Maslow, 1968). In a boundary violation, the dismantling of clients' safety strikes at the core of their security. Not only must they face the terror of having been alone and defenseless in the relationship, but they also suffer a deep and lasting injury to their soul, for the betrayal of their trust threatens the beliefs with which they anchor themselves in the world. Indeed, they may lose their belief in the ancient and biblical covenant of fidelity that allows them to turn over their well-being to professionals and to feel safe in doing so. The damage to this spiritual process has far-reaching implications. A client described how she maintains a distance after having been exploited by her minister, who, in addition to numerous other invasions, manipulated her dependency through the misuse of sacraments:

> This minister said she would help me quit smoking. She performed various ceremonial rituals which included anointing my head with holy oil early in the morning so that I could gain

strength from the sacraments to go through the day and not smoke. It felt incredibly nurturing.

I was terribly addicted to nicotine. As I started to withdraw, I kind of fell apart and things got really upsetting. I know now that I was dealing with chemical dependency. This minister, however, said I should do a general confession. She had me go with her to a dark chapel at night and tell her all this stuff about my entire life. It was unbelievably intense. The only light was from candles. I remember crying while she hugged me and told me that I had been sexually abused. She even told me how her father had violated her. As long as we stayed religious it was okay, but messing with my sexual past was really terrifying.

I left the church for a long time and began to meditate with members of the Bahai faith. The sacraments are meaningless to me. I don't understand the fuss about communion anymore. I have not opened a Bible since. I haven't met a minister I like since all this happened. Not one. I kind of like this new minister I met, but I don't really trust her. I don't feel like being close to her. I don't know if I can ever have a normal relationship with a minister, just a normal, steady relationship. It's a lifelong battle to maintain some integrity and some kind of intimacy with others that's safe.

Whether clients are in danger or not, they continue to feel afraid. Although they want to feel safe again, letting go and trusting people or situations that could be dangerous seems like an insurmountable task. They therefore shield themselves by avoiding whatever scares them. While avoidance protects clients from reexperiencing fear, the cost for this protection is high. They frequently sacrifice or compromise other needs so that they can attend to their safety first. A client who had had a vasectomy shared his reluctance to return to his physician or to see any others:

The operation was described as being virtually painless. When I complained that it hurt, the doctor argued that he would rather cut the right things than the wrong things. Later he asked me if he could get a discount at the clothing store where I worked. He said, "You know I have your balls in one hand and a scalpel in the other hand and you ought to be telling me that you'll give me anything I want for free." I didn't say anything to him. I just dropped the subject. I didn't know if he was causing me pain intentionally or because he was incompetent. Since he had totally dismissed my earlier complaints, I was concerned that the operation could become even more painful.

It was two weeks before I could walk normally and spend a regular day at work. It's been many months and I haven't been back for a sperm count. My wife keeps taking birth control pills because she doesn't feel certain about the success of the vasectomy.

In addition to physically retreating, many clients protect themselves by psychologically withdrawing. Believing they were made vulnerable by a false sense of security, they adopt a fundamental position of distrust as a way to blanketly defend against any possible recurrence. They falsely believe that they can reclaim control of their destiny by withholding their trust.

This decision, however, makes them prisoners of their own fear. Since they cannot erase their needs or regulate all of what comes at them, they limit how they respond and retreat inside themselves. To the extent that they shrink internally, they cut off contact with the outside world. Their sole goal becomes self-preservation. They replace the spiritual base that once gave them hope with suspicion and cynicism. They replace critical thinking with fear. They replace trust with hypervigilance.

While this new style of adaptation affords some protection, the overall cost to clients is high. Indeed, clients' efforts to help themselves often actually cripple them further. By hiding themselves to stay safe, clients are not free to live as fully as possible. For example, a student who was abused by a teacher may sit in the back of classrooms to avoid being

seen. While making himself "invisible" may permit him to feel safer, it
also may stunt his ability to concentrate and understand the material
because he cannot hear or see as well. Moreover, clients who view their
future relationships with professionals through a filter of paranoia skew
reality and cut themselves off from whatever protection and safety they
could have. This state of ready alert actually causes clients to re-expe-
rience the fear from the original trauma, which etches itself even deeper
into their psyche. Their sense of danger persists, their needs are relegated
to a lower priority, and the violation still controls how they function. A
client described how she retreated after her therapist purchased insurance from her company and used her as his agent:

> The therapy was over from the day he bought the insurance.
> When I went to see him after that, I couldn't really truly express to
> him my feelings because I didn't feel comfortable. Yet I didn't want
> to totally quit seeing him because he was helping me with the
> problems of being a single parent. So I only talked about my son.
> I'm real good at storing things and not expressing myself. He didn't
> know half my problems. While I went through the motions of
> going there, I felt defeated half the time. Since I couldn't get help, I
> felt like a failure and lived like a recluse for a long time.

Attempts to avoid potentially dangerous, stressful situations have serious, long-term implications for clients. Those who are in inescapable
situations are particularly susceptible to being harmed by the very methods they use to ensure their safety. A client who had married her debate
coach described how their relationship affected her passivity and ability
to think critically:

> My professor mentored me, advised me, and told me which
> classes to take. It was a situation where I had to have my decisions
> validated. Either you got it right or you got it wrong. The whole
> relationship was unequal. He was the big, important older person

who had the answers and I was the little girl who didn't. He used to say proudly, "If you marry them young, you raise them right."

The decisions about my career were not really my own. I laugh whenever someone asks why I chose teaching. I didn't choose it. He picked it. In fact, I set my life at a second level because he made the first-level decisions for me. I couldn't develop my own ability to judge because if I did, it meant I was being critical of him. I stayed safe in the marriage by not arguing.

I have tremendous difficulty evaluating my own work today. I never developed the eyes to see my own performance for myself. As a teacher, I still struggle with critically evaluating other people's work. It is easier to buy into their process, their assumptions, and their conclusions than to challenge why they made the assumptions they did. The freedom to challenge is what makes a student-teacher relationship healthy. That's how growth happens. That's the scariest and the hardest part for me. I tend to always back down.

Backing off as a way to manage fear merely produces an uneasy calm. The mechanisms that clients use to create a sanctuary inside actually entrap them further. By generalizing the pattern of avoidance, clients unconsciously fixate on the violation, which keeps it alive and powerful until finally it becomes the organizing principle in their lives. They cannot feel truly safe again because they are too frightened to risk the unknown. (The influence of prior abuse on the client's adaptive responses is discussed in the section entitled "Populations with Special Vulnerabilities.")

Blocks to Gaining Control

The ability of people to manage their personal world is key to their feeling strong and competent. While the specific consequences of a boundary violation may be damaging, nothing matches the abject terror that flows when clients juxtapose the professional's power over them and the capriciousness of his or her actions against their own lack of awareness in the relationship. Acknowledgment of this level of helplessness returns clients to a childlike state of dependency and defenselessness. Consequently, they go to great lengths to ward off the truth of their victimization, a truth that would further undo and debilitate them. A client admitted his reluctance when he said, "It would be awfully hard for me to admit my attorney was fifty times more in control than I was, to believe that he was just using me. Would that mean he was smarter than me? Does that make me stupid?"

Another client shared her conflict with herself as she struggled to accept what happened to her and other clients who were hurt by a therapist:

> I fight knowing the full size of what happened. I don't want to acknowledge my helplessness. I think I could forgive myself more if I could really say there was nothing I could have done. I know that everybody else did the best they could at that point in time. While I believe it for them, I don't always believe it for me.

While both of these clients can almost taste the relief they would feel if they would begin mapping the way out for themselves, their need to hold back the tidal wave of their vulnerability still takes precedence for them, as it does for many other clients. It is simply too overwhelming for them to face the arbitrary nature of events, their delusions about a just and orderly world, and their lack of protection against impending danger.

Clients often defend against the ensuing despair by taking responsibility for the violation. If they can think of themselves as having caused it, what happened makes more sense. Moreover, they can feel more in control, stronger, and more instrumental in determining their destiny. Unfortunately, their sense of empowerment is twisted in the process. Their acceptance of responsibility for the violation skews reality, distorts the relationship, and leaves them with a false sense of their power. A client described how she condemned herself for responding to an advance from her minister:

> So much of my life I've given in. If I get pushed hard enough, I just decide it's not really that important. I'm going to end up having sex some day with someone anyway. So I told myself, "Why not have it be with him because he loves me? Why not just do it and get it over with?" I relented. So once again, it was me saying yes. It made me feel in control so that I didn't feel raped. I felt like I was in charge and that made me feel better at the time. In trying to work this all through, the last thing for me to let go of was the belief that I was in control.

Like this woman, many clients see themselves as willing participants in the violation. They confuse consent with compliance. •

Consent is an misnomer. In order for a noncoercive relationship to occur, consent has to be informed, mutual, and meaningful (Fortune, 1989). "Consent" means to agree, to be of the same mind, or to give permission. "Informed" means that all of the possible risks and consequences have been communicated and understood. "Mutual" means that the power in the relationship is equal. "Meaningful" means that the patient can say no without the possibility of harmful consequences to self, the treatment, or the relationship. Clearly, the unequal power balance in the relationship and the omnipresent threat of consequences to the client makes full consent impossible. Even so, clients maintain the illusion of their voluntary involvement because it gives them a feeling of control.

Unfortunately, these attempts to reduce helplessness lock clients into a never ending spiral of self-condemnation. They feel ashamed for having needs. They feel responsible for and guilty about how they behaved in the relationship. Indeed, they make what happened in the relationship logical by determining that they provoked, participated in, or were deserving of the abuse. Some clients feel like fools. While smarting from having been double-crossed, they transfer their anger at the professional to themselves and call themselves stupid for letting themselves be manipulated. Some clients feel ashamed of who they are. They believe the violation happened because they are bad and therefore deserving of punishment. Following this irrational logic, they condemn themselves for "being" while justifying the rightness of the professional's mistreatment.

Some clients feel like losers. They blame themselves for their neediness. Feeling inferior and abnormal, they call themselves a failure because they became the object of the professional's attention. As one client said, "If I hadn't needed so much, it wouldn't have happened."

As clients fault themselves for their needs or their human responses, they convince themselves that they had choices and were self-determining in the relationship. Sadly, this belief is reinforced by some professionals who espouse the philosophy of equality and mutuality that was the core of the humanistic movement that influenced all five professions during the 1970s. According to this approach, the professional-client relationship is a partnership in which the professional follows the client's lead in making decisions. The relationship, which is deliberately structured to ignore the power differential, gives the client the illusion of control. Unfortunately, it also inflicts a harsh punishment. The shame for just "being" and the guilt about their behavior impose a silence that leaves clients thrashing in a pit of self-directed contemptuousness and self-hatred. Such castigation merely excuses the professional and diminishes the immorality of the violation itself.

Blocks to Gaining Validation

The very privacy that marks the professional-client relationship also isolates victimized clients, promotes secrecy about the violation, and limits verification of the professional's misbehavior. Since the wound is invisible, clients question the credibility of their experience. Without outside support, they deny their reality and minimize the violation. Out of loyalty or indebtedness to the professional, they look the other way. The shame and guilt imprison them in their aloneness.

If and when clients decide to break their silence, they search out friends and family or other professionals who can help. They hope that telling their story will relieve their pain and isolation. They seek validation for their feelings and permission to rejoin the wider community. All too often, however, clients are dismissed and subjected to a powerful backlash from the people they approach. A client described the reaction she received when she approached the client security board to get back the money her attorney had stolen from her trust account:

> So many people made me feel guilty. They blamed me by saying, "Why didn't you investigate him?" "Why weren't you checking up on him?" "Why weren't you making him accountable?" I totally trusted this man. He had treated me like a daughter. To have done that would have been like going to my dad and asking him what he was doing with my money. I wouldn't dream of questioning him. You just assume your father is looking after you. Nobody understood that. I felt responsible for what had happened. I know I'm not, but I still feel that way.

Like this woman, clients often receive messages that the violation happened because of who they are and what they did. It is common that the behavior of a client is scrutinized *first*, which places greater emphasis and more weight on the person who in fact has less power in the relationship. Clients have their "psychopathology" critiqued. They may be faulted for their compliance. They may be accused of malicious and vindictive motives. Thus, rather than gaining support, clients frequently feel even more ostracized and alone. A client described how her family physician used his knowledge about her family to predict what her mother's reaction would be if she revealed that he had abused her:

When I was an adolescent, my mother and I had an argument and I locked myself in my room. My mother called the doctor, told him I was hysterical, and asked him to come to the house and give me a sedative. She told him I was very sensitive. He knew that my mom wouldn't listen to me. Later, when he abused me in his office, I screamed at him that I was going to tell my mother. I remember he said, "She won't listen to you anyway." When I did tell her, she didn't believe me. All she said was, "Oh, you're just too sensitive." I argued and said, "No, Mom. There is something wrong." But I didn't get through to her and I wound up just giving up.

Clients' attempts to cope are often viewed as symptoms of pathology rather than as efforts to stave off or manage the consequences of the trauma. All too often, clients mistakenly (and sometimes conveniently) diagnosed as having borderline personality disorder, anxiety disorder, dysthymia, or paranoia are actually suffering from post-traumatic stress caused by a boundary violation. In fact, their difficulties with reality-testing, affective regulation, impulse control, self-integration, and interpersonal relationships may be positive strivings to adapt to the effects of the violation and the lack of its resolution.

By emphasizing the client's behavior, others minimize the professional's responsibility and indirectly blame the client for his or her pain. The asymmetry in the relationship is further distorted when they rationalize or excuse the professional's misconduct. Professionals may be exempted on the basis that the violation happened outside their professional sphere of responsibility or did not interfere with the performance of their professional duties. Moreover, their behavior may be recast and explained away as "problems in communication" or dismissed as idiosyncratic and, therefore, inconsequential. A client described what happened when she approached a therapist's supervisor about the therapist's unsolicited telephone calls and inappropriate behavior:

[handwritten margin note: check for boundary violations first!]

It was very hard for me to talk to this man. Though I liked him and he was open, I was expecting a little more shock, surprise, or alarm when I told him what the therapist had done. This supervisor didn't want to label it as inappropriate. He defended the therapist. He essentially said, "Don't worry. I'm sure he's not making advances. This is just his style. This is the way he is. He's kind of informal." He didn't make me feel I was wrong necessarily, but he did not support me either.

In addition to exonerating the professional, family and friends or other professionals may even attack clients for telling the truth because it causes trouble. Clients are given the message that their pain is not as great as the pain they could cause the professional. A client reported how her advisor reacted when she told him about being harassed by an instructor: "My God," he said, "if you tell people about that, you could ruin his promising career!"

Such reactions are common. Other professionals often identify with the fallibility of a colleague who is being singled out. Acting out of their own self-interests, many of them divorce themselves from their responsibility for the situation or for attending to clients' needs. Their stance of neutrality is often predicated on the theory that the client and the professional are equal opponents. Their lack of involvement not only distorts the power imbalance but also leaves clients to carry the pain of the violation alone.

DAMAGE TO THIRD PARTIES

If a client suffers no harmful consequences or does not have enough information to be aware of a boundary violation, he or she may have no response. However, a third party or subordinate to the professional may be emotionally affected by the professional's failure to take responsibility for the violation. In having to keep the secret, the third party may well internalize the shame that belongs to the professional. A legal assistant described her reaction to the legal decisions made by an attorney specializing in medical malpractice:

> This man wields his power and gets lost in the control. He obsesses and strategizes over every tiny fact. He researches a subject to the nth degree or gets every expert possible to say this is what is true. He is known as an excellent attorney who has all the facts and can blow anybody out of the water. Since a trial is an unsure situation and you cannot control every sentence that comes out of someone's mouth, this attorney resolves his terror by never going to trial. Instead, he settles. He convinces the physicians that settling is the best solution, by saying that a trial would mean they would have to be away from their practices for two weeks and they might not win, and that all their dirty laundry would be aired in front of the community. He also tells them that even though they did nothing wrong, there is a sympathy factor in favor of the patient and the jury is going to go with the plaintiff. This attorney justifies what he is doing to others by saying "Why would we want to go to trial when we could settle it for $100,000 and a trial would cost us $200,000?"
>
> I feel bad for the clients who have judgments against them on their records. If they had gone to trial, that might not have been the result. Furthermore, the client's insurance goes up.

A nurse described how she internalized the violation and carried the pain of it when a physician denied his involvement in the critical care of a patient:

> I was doing rounds when I came upon a patient who was having chest pain. I called the doctor in the middle of the night. I voiced my concerns about this patient, who was the mother of his receptionist. The doctor had been drinking and was upset that I had called. He told me to give the patient a particular medication and call back in twenty minutes. Ten minutes later, the patient died. First I called the resuscitation team and then I called the

physician. He said he wasn't coming in just to handle this situation. The next morning the doctor came barging in, furious that he had not been notified.

I have no doubt that he had had a blackout and didn't remember my phone calls. He questioned my competence, and I had to fill out an incident report about what I had done wrong. For two years I had nightmares about passing out meds and making errors. I would go in half an hour early to work. Since I worried that I was dyslexic and might write down the wrong thing, I would use colored pens to mark the treatments prescribed for the patients and carried that sheet of paper with me at all times. I got into checking myself again and again. Since I felt I was at risk for making mistakes, I had to make sure I knew absolutely everything.

Clearly, third parties are secondary victims of the violation. They are trapped by their concern for clients, their subservient position to the professional, and their concern for themselves. Like clients who take care of the professional, these individuals all too often protect the professional by keeping the secret. They also are double-bound: To implicate the professional might cost them their jobs; yet to remain silent makes them a co-conspirator in the violation. Like clients who speak up, those who decide to blow the whistle are frequently ostracized and condemned. A therapist described the reaction of other personnel when she refused to work with a colleague who was abusing clients:

> Nobody challenged the inappropriateness of my colleague's behavior. After I spoke up, people chose not to include me in things. No one talked to me about it. It was like it didn't happen. I know I was talked about and my boundaries were seen as rigid. Only one person put a note in my box saying she respected me for the very difficult decision that I needed to make, but she never said anything to my face. Later, one of the clients who had been abused decided to sue my colleague and the agency. My supervisor called

me in and said, "I want you to know that I hold you responsible for this lawsuit and the loss of several thousand dollars. If you hadn't been talking, nobody would know what happened."

POPULATIONS WITH SPECIAL VULNERABILITIES

Any client is potentially at risk for boundary violations, as well as for internalizing the damage. Certain clients are particularly at risk, however, because of factors in their history or belief system that exacerbate their vulnerability and affect how they feel they are "allowed" to respond to violations. Like other victimized clients, they suffer the pain of the violation and the professional's failure to accept responsibility. Unfortunately, they suffer even more if they attempt to address the violation, because doing so means they have to confront the factors that contributed to their victimization.

Impact of Gender Socialization

Gender differences in psychic structure are the result of social role conditioning. In *The Reproduction of Mothering*, Nancy Chodorow (1978) explained that women value attachment, rapport, and affinity because their care was provided primarily by women. Since men are required as children to renounce their attachment and similarity to "mother," they are forced to choose separateness and independence to be other than who she is. They therefore diminish the significance of the relationship and move away from it.

This difference is further elaborated by Carol Gilligan (1982), whose book, *In a Different Voice*, examined the contrast between men and women in their responses to moral dilemmas. Because female identity is rooted in connection and relationships, women's responses emphasize the ethic of care and responsibility. Because male identity is rooted in autonomy and self-reliance, men's responses emphasize fairness and rights.

Not surprisingly, the reactions of women and men to a boundary violation are also powerfully influenced by gender dynamics. Women tend to take on the whole of it ("I'm to blame"). Men are validated for their denial of it ("It didn't happen"). Both scripts help normalize professionals' misconduct and maintain the status quo.

Women in particular are subject to feeling responsible for relationships and for meeting the needs of others to the exclusion of their own. In surveys of sexual exploitation of clients by professionals, the vulnerability of women is pronounced, in that predominantly the victims are female and the professionals male (Kuchan, 1989). Indeed, when something goes wrong, women frequently endure the situation and "instinctively" blame themselves or look for a way to fix it. Primed to believe that they matter because of what they do for others, they easily fall into the position of caretaker and wait for others to define their rights. Rather than risk rejection, they are apt to discount their perceptions and to believe instead that what professionals do is right, necessary, and acceptable. Women tend to filter reality through this mindset, which distorts the issue of responsibility and numbs their anger.

A client shared a letter she had written her priest after he hugged her and sent her a $100 check for listening to his problems into the wee hours of the morning:

> Father Francis,
> I received your card today and the check. I'm sorry but I cannot accept that from you. I realize you're very lonely right now and want a friend, but I'm beginning to feel very uncomfortable about how you are interpreting things. I know you're very depressed and feel like you're losing all your friends, but I feel it would be best not to see each other for a while. Maybe during this time you might be able to get things worked out. Don't be afraid to go see a

counselor. I'd like to see things get better for you, and I think having someone to talk to like a counselor would be really good for you. Don't be afraid of getting help. I have enclosed the check you sent. I cannot accept something like that.

While this woman drew the boundary and protected herself, she concealed her anger from the professional, did not act on it, and expressed it only in her journal:

I feel so betrayed by him, especially since he's taken a vow. The way he was holding me was so uncomfortable and he wouldn't let go. I feel so cheap since he sent that money. I feel like he was paying me for services. Does he think I'm a whore? It makes me so angry that he thinks I would even consider it. Why wouldn't he appreciate the friendship I was offering?

Because they are taught to be selfless, women who experience boundary violations struggle with issues of self-worth. ⟩

Men, in contrast, are apt to deny what has happened because acknowledging abuse emasculates them. Since a "true" male is strong and independent, a man who is vulnerable, helpless, and unable to protect himself is more like a woman and therefore less. To maintain his masculinity, he rejects the truth of the violation, closes off his feelings, and pretends to be other than who he is. Unfortunately, these seemingly self-protective maneuvers leave him at greater risk because he can only protect himself by ignoring what has happened.

Having worked for foundations, an MBA student described his hesitancy to concede that he had been violated when his teacher asked him to use his expertise to procure a grant for the department:

I viewed my professor as an exceedingly fine teacher and person, but I found myself in an impossible scene that I couldn't coordinate. I went in and out of different psychic states depending on whether I was a student or a professional. It was incompatible to both advise and teach my teacher at the same time that he was teaching me. Even to this day I get a slight nervous twitch when I think of that process. I'm glad I did it, but I wasn't aware of what I was doing to myself.

It still doesn't register that he violated me. I can't admit it. I viewed myself as older than he was. I could have avoided it by just saying it's not appropriate. I could have said no. I reject the idea of a violation without examining it because it just can't happen. I know too much. I'm an older person. I'm a wise person. I've lived a long time and I've learned a lot so that wouldn't happen to me. Besides, I don't want him to feel bad for doing it, so I make what was going on inside of me not as significant.

In our society, both men and women are socialized in ways that make it difficult for them to interpret or react to violations as being abusive. For women to pay attention to their victimization, they must drop their interpersonal orientation, which is socially prescribed. For men to pay attention to their victimization, they must drop their impenetrable mask and their seeming independence, which are also socially mandated.

Impact of Prior Abuse

Violence is increasingly recognized as pervasive throughout our culture and the world. In the United States, for example, 38% of all female children have been sexually assaulted before the age of 18. A 1984 study found that 43% of patients discharged over an 18-month period from a psychiatric inpatient unit had histories of physical or sexual abuse. A 1986 study found that in a nonalcoholic control group of women, 50% reported sexual abuse, 34% reported physical abuse, and 44% reported emotional abuse. Moreover, the study indicated that acts of violence are highest among people who know each other. For example, 65% of the 50% nonalcoholic, sexually abused women were violated before age 10, 82% of the 43% nonalcoholic, physically abused women were violated before age 10, and 100% of the 44% nonalcoholic emotionally abused women were violated before age 10. It is assumed—given the age of the victims—that most of the abuse occurred within the family or was by someone already present in the child's life (Covington, 1986).

Given these high indices, it is common for many clients who are victims of boundary violations to have a history of prior abuse. In recounting how a physician had been inappropriate with her as an adult, a client spontaneously remembered having been abused as a child:

> We had a real old-fashioned doctor in town. One time I went in for a sore throat and he told me to unbutton my blouse. I felt it was real inappropriate for what I went in there for. I went home and told my mom about it. She said, "He's got that reputation, but just ignore it. He's old." I was only 14. When you're that age, you don't have much choice about whom you go to see, but I never went back to him again. I must have gotten some message about normalizing what happened from my mother. I feel it must have made an impact on me somewhere.

Many clients come from families in which boundaries are underdeveloped, that is, dysfunctional families. Consequently, they have problems differentiating appropriate from inappropriate behavior. In fact, confusion about roles and responsibilities is commonplace. Replaying histories of chronic betrayal, they normalize the hurt and therefore do not realize that they are in danger. Having no recognition or a distorted understanding of boundaries while feeling needy in the company of a caring and concerned professional, they may unconsciously behave in ways that "encourage" the violation or may be too responsive to the professional when others would be on guard. A client described the environment of chaos and violence in her family and how it was replicated in her relationship with her minister:

> At the age of six, I stood between my mom and my dad, who had a gun. Dad was a violent alcoholic. A lot of physical abuse between my parents resulted in their divorce. I got very sick and

ended up in the hospital. The pastor came to visit me every day. He took on the job of rescuer and I suddenly got all this attention.

About a year later, he started to touch me. He would talk to me about my dad and how bad and evil he was. He didn't want me to see him. He tried to teach me about the bad ways of the world and bad people. I didn't always understand what he was talking about. I just knew it made me hurt and it made me real sad. Then he would comfort me by being sexual.

I grew up with a sense that I was an innately evil person, with the minister defining what was good and bad. I believed I was being punished for having sinned. That was the reality in my family and that was the reality in the church. To even believe there was another reality was crazy. To me, abuse was normal.

Since many clients have figured out ways to psychologically manage childhood abuse, it is often difficult for them to sort out whether or not their reaction to the current situation is part of a lifelong adaptation or a specific response to the violation itself. Therapists who try to help such clients also wrestle with uncovering the source of their reaction. If they determine it derives from previous abuse or is a part of their core personality structure, they may discount the current abuse. If they determine that the cause of the disturbance is the violation, they may not go deeply enough into clients' core issues to stimulate change. Clients with a history of prior abuse are therefore vulnerable because they cannot identify or respond self-protectively to potentially dangerous situations. They are also likely to receive inadequate help because therapists, too, cannot ascertain what fits where.

Impact of Membership in a Closed System

Some clients encounter professionals who adhere to a rigid system built around the personality of the leader or a political ideology. Seeing themselves as the "only real experts," these professionals close themselves off from the checks and balances that might otherwise help them guard against boundary violations. They give clients an idiosyncratic system of rules to follow. Since these rules are presented as ethical stances, the arbitrary and self-serving nature of these professionals' prescriptions cannot be seen by clients. Moreover, these professionals discourage any critical thinking on the part of their clients. Any questioning becomes iconoclastic and results in clients' being shamed into obedience. Clients therefore are forced to choose between their sanity and membership in the system.

When professionals deny the power differential and replace it with an ideology of equality, the boundary that protects clients from being exploited is erased. Likewise, professionals whose loyalty to a given ideology supersedes their loyalty to clients are apt to mandate compliance and conformity, thereby abrogating their clients' right to question them about their practices. Unfortunately, many clients, in looking for an external guide, are attracted to professionals and client groups who profess a compelling allegiance to such doctrines. Clients who accept these pseudo ethics are usually ignorant of their far-reaching implications. A woman described the self-destructiveness of her loyalty to her physician and his fasting program for overweight women:

> This clinic was the only place in town that had a fasting program and I was ready to do anything to get the weight off. The physician asked me if I was willing to give up my marriage to get the weight off. He said, "Usually when women are very heavy and they lose a lot of weight, it ends their relationship. You have to decide if you will give it up before I can put you on this program." I had to say yes. Everything the doctor said, I accepted. I wanted my husband to accept it too so that he wouldn't mess up my weight loss. I was incredibly naive.
>
> The doctor wanted me to work for him but not until I got more weight off. He told me we'd be great friends when I had the

weight off. I felt chosen. At the same time, he would drink Coke by the gallons and eat chocolate candy bars in front of me. He told me he had to eat all the time to keep weight on his bones. All I was drinking was water and cherry juice. The fasting made me so vulnerable. And I couldn't stay on the diet. I'd have incredible shame because I would fast for five days and then I'd eat. It was real bulimic behavior.

For nine months, I gave up all kinds of things just to keep seeing him because it was the only way I could get the weight off. He encouraged my belief that fasting was the only answer.

Frequently, the ideology of a program is shared and supported by a group of clients. The idealization of the leader, the elitism of the group, and the influence of the crowd make it easy for individual clients to ignore their own reality. Many groups that are bonded to specific religious, political, gender, or healing agendas contain an element of hostility directed against the outside world. Since the group forms "in opposition to," attention is easily directed away from internal violations and toward the common enemy that binds the members together.

When members are violated, they are dissuaded from their normal healthy reactions, which are construed as pathological or as evidence of oppressive political conditioning. Rather than question and risk the enmity of the professional or the group, they are likely to cling to their membership and the personal meaning the group gives to their lives. A client described her sense of captivity in a therapy group, the numerous violations that occurred there, and the treatment philosophy that was used to justify unorthodox practices:

My spouse and I were in therapy with a married team of counselors who were therapists. It was as if they were the parents and we were the kids. There were right answers and wrong answers, and they rephrased everything in their lingo. If you didn't agree with them, you were out. These therapists would share confidential information about their clients and talk against them behind their backs. They had us house-sit in exchange for counseling. We slept in their bed. They got off on how we were like them and asked if we fit the right grooves in the mattress. We spent a lot of time in their home socializing. We were trying to fit in and be them. It was bizarre. My anxiety was always sky-high.

They were very crafty, intelligent, and charismatic. They felt they were a cut above the rest of the community because they had the answers figured out. They told us that since we didn't get what we needed as children, we should be fed, stroked, and loved so that the holes inside us could heal up. For two hours at a time, one of the therapists would hold me with my head on her breast. She would tell me to relax and gave me a bottle of whatever I wanted to drink. I felt like I was too close to her. It wasn't appropriate. It didn't feel right, but I kept thinking something was wrong with me because I couldn't relax.

I have some shame about being involved with these yo-yos. Now that I'm out of the cloud of their power and in broad daylight, the whole thing sounds bizarre. People must wonder how an intelligent person could slip into this, but I recognize that I was in a vulnerable state. I would be understanding of anyone who told this story because I now realize that this kind of stuff is possible.

Clients who are members of closed systems are especially vulnerable because they are more blocked than usual from their ability to be self-determining. Unless they can break the hold of the professional, group, or ideology on their psyche, they cannot exercise their free will.

The Impaired Recovery of the Client

The victims of boundary violations are made additionally defenseless by gender-prescribed roles and responses, childhood abuse, and group norms. While they know they are stuck, they are frequently unaware of how these powerful influences work against them. Extricating themselves from the violation may mean they have to open the door to additional pain as they examine their allegiance to self-defeating patterns and/or repressed memories of childhood abuse.

Client reactions to boundary violations vary considerably. While all victimized clients feel some degree of disbelief and loss, some clearly suffer more than others. Clearly sexual violations leave deep, ugly scars. Seemingly less serious abuse can also produce long-lasting damage as the flow of clients' lives is interrupted.

In all instances, a violation begins as a wound to the relationship. Since its consequences are felt only by clients, the violation moves from its external source inward into their psyche and so becomes viewed, however incorrectly, as their problem. Once internalized, the violation has continuing impact. It festers and churns, infecting any important decisions clients make about arenas related to the violation.

Since a violation is a relational injury, it can never be fully resolved by clients alone. The "stuckness" of clients reflects the displacement of the violation. Clients are frustrated in their efforts to master their pain because they carry what does not belong to them. Handicapped by the professional's absence, their efforts to resolve the violation remain incomplete. Moreover, these same efforts intensify the damage. Until they can answer the question why, clients cannot fully comprehend and assimilate what happened. The professional's acknowledgment and cooperation are critical to the healing process.

VI

HEALING: REDRAWING
THE BOUNDARY

ALL OF THE MORALLY AND ETHICALLY based professions are bonded to the covenant of life. Whatever their specific activities may be, professionals are compelled and obliged to do work that is life-enhancing. When a boundary violation occurs, however, the reverence for life which connects the professional to the client is aborted. With the attachment between them ripped apart, each feels an even deeper rip inside that comes from the shared knowledge that the professional did something to diminish life rather than affirm it.

Once clients become aware of how they were wronged, they naturally experience compassion for themselves and anger toward the professional. If left to seek its own level, their anger leads them to revenge. Once professionals become aware of what they did, they naturally experience terror about the future. If left to seek its own level, their terror leads them to give the highest priority to their self-protection. While both these proclivities are normal and provide short-term relief, they are not life-affirming. Indeed, revenge and the terror that drives the need for self-protection are poisoning forces that jeopardize life. To resist the pull to polarize their positions on these grounds, professionals and clients must choose a path that is not defined by the other but instead is delineated by what each must do for himself or herself to repair the rip each feels inside.

Although the paths for professionals and clients may be parallel, what must be resolved is different for each of them. Clients have to connect with their core self and their outrage. Professionals have to connect with their personal neediness and the truth about what happened.

These are soul-searching and existential journeys. Life expands as clients and professionals develop greater self-awareness. As they have more of themselves, they have what they need to rejoin the larger community. They also have what they need to mend the wound between them. Indeed, their reverence for their own truth and their belief that speaking it will be healing allow them to come together at the center of what happened.

reclaiming self

HEALING THE CORE SELF OF THE CLIENT

For many clients, the pain from the violation stays deep inside. Having adjusted their lives to maintain their safety, such clients push the injury into the recesses of their minds. While they are occasionally reminded of the hurt, normalizing what they have had to do to accommodate the violation allows them to minimize and dismiss the damage. For other clients, the pain stays closer to the surface and interrupts their functioning. As a result, their efforts at denial are less effective, and they are forced to do more to stop their suffering. Their journey is arduous. They discover they have to endure even more pain, face many hard truths, and let go of their search for clarity and answers if they are to heal the original hurt and get on with their lives.

Removing Fault, Feeling Robbed, Finding Anger

To externalize the pain, clients have to challenge the responsibility they falsely assumed for the violation and the logic they used to establish causation. As one client said about himself in relation to a therapist who had emotionally abused him, "Since everyone else was surprised that this therapist had acted the way he did with me, I decided it had happened because I hadn't trusted him enough." For clients to grasp that the violation happened *to* them and not because of them, they must relinquish their certainty about what they believe is true. They have to give up their critical and self-condemning assumptions that they provoked the violation or contributed to it because they were stupid, said the wrong thing, wore the wrong clothes, did not listen to others, should have known better, or should not have been so needy or dependent. They have to understand that they were and still are mistaken in how they add up the situation and make sense of the world.

Realizing that they do not perceive reality accurately sets them adrift. It causes more anxiety because they see how little control they had. It creates yet another crisis because now they feel they cannot trust either the outside world or their own perceptions.

Modifying their impaired logic and waking to these realities is often a slow and gradual process. Clients may delay because their search triggers memories of other painful incidents in their lives for which, by using the same faulty reasoning, they held themselves liable for their own victimization. They may not want or be able to cope with the intensity or unacceptability of the feelings that follow. If and when they press on, they come to realize that their perceptions of the world kept them from acknowledging they were robbed of their rights, dignity, and self-worth. This realization brings more loss. They then have to grieve how much time they wasted as a result of their self-imposed emotional imprisonment, what was taken, and what was destroyed. They have to mourn the

importance of
mourning what has
been lost or violated!

144   AT PERSONAL RISK

loss of their belief that it was safe to trust the individual professional and
the loss of their innocence. A woman who was abused by a female
minister described her pain when the truth about their relationship
broke through: "I cried from a place that I didn't know I even had. I felt
like an abandoned baby left to fend for myself on the streets somewhere.
I have never cried before or since from wherever those feelings came
from."

Thankfully, becoming aware of their faulty thinking also brings the
balm of self-compassion clients so sorely need. As they grieve for themselves and can allow their injury to stand fully exposed and undistorted,
they reattach to their core sense of being deserving human beings and
discover the self-love that can restore their sense of worth. Moreover,
when connected to their tenderness for themselves, they gain access to
the feelings that can energize, ground, and enable them to take self-
protective measures. More specifically, their compassion gives them access to their anger.

Clients' acceptance that nothing they did warranted their mistreatment allows them to feel the injustice of the violation and claim what
was rightfully owed them in the relationship. By knowing where to
place the blame, they feel stronger and more confident in their ability to
advocate for themselves. A client described finding her anger after a
therapist verbally abused her:

> When I got out of the office, I started to cry. I was shaking and
> thinking, "This is what she really thinks of me. I'm just pathetic. I
> can't stop eating. My whole life is a mess. It's not worth it." For a
> while, I sat in my car unable to drive. When I got home, I thought
> it over and said to myself, "Hey, what just happened to you was
> like abuse." I recognized it! After many years in therapy and the
> thousands of dollars I spent to learn about abuse, I know that
> abusers are abusers and it's not something magical about me that
> turns them on. Pretending the therapist was there, I said, "Don't

take your big load of problems and smear them all over me. Just have them back."

Through expressing their anger, clients find the clarity they initially sought in their attempt to understand the violation. They realize it comes not from figuring out the professional's intent or which of the dual realities was true but rather from believing in themselves and honoring their sense of outrage.

Confronting the Professional

Anger empowers clients to fight for themselves. Feeling more generous toward themselves and less shameful about what happened, they can then seek to change their feelings of diminishment and invisibility by standing up to the professional. To take back what was stolen and to reestablish their self-worth, they realize, at some level, that they have to come out of the shadows of their self-protective isolation and disclose their story to the world. Letting their reality matter that much, however, makes them vulnerable once again to this powerful person who, because of his or her credentials, is automatically granted stature in the community. Not only must they sever their primary loyalty to the professional, but they also must break the rules of silence and secrecy that have kept the cancer of the violation contained. Going public, therefore, produces terror, because to do so clients have to give up more control.

The decision to confront the professional arises from clients' conviction that (1) telling their story will give credence to their experience and (2) holding the professional accountable for the violation will help release them so that they can move forward with their lives. Before taking this step, however, clients have to be honest with themselves about their motives, readiness, and expectations. If they are not clear about where they stand in relation to these three important considerations, they place themselves at risk for more pain.

Knowing their purpose in confronting the professional is critical for clients because it directs their decisions about their behavior. As already stated, it is not uncommon for clients to funnel their newly found anger into a desire for revenge. In fact, clients often want to make as painful an impact on the professional as he or she made on them. However, if they put their energy into getting even instead of getting better, they keep the violation alive. While evening the score may be immediately satisfying, it is always short-lived. Indeed, since clients' vengeful actions do not emerge out of a fundamental allegiance to their own growth and recovery, their attempts to "win" by defeating the professional keep them bound to the professional and also in pain. A client described how far she went to get a therapist to admit her mistakes and how unfinished she felt afterward. This particular therapist had crossed a number of boundaries by inappropriately disclosing personal information about herself and behaving in ways that the client interpreted as a come-on:

> My therapist wasn't open to being honest about her part of the problem. When she told me that she was finished and that I therefore needed to leave, I walked into the bathroom and wrote her a note. It was the angriest note I had ever written. In it, I said, "I hate you. I hate your guts." I slid it under her door and then kicked the door because I wanted to make noise. I filed a grievance against her with her professional organization. At this point, I'm not sure what else I'm going to do. I have the options of filing a legal case and filing a complaint with the state board of licensing.
>
> I don't want to do either of those things, however, because I don't think they'll help me. Filing the complaint with the professional association doesn't seem to make any difference. Instead, I need to sit down and confront her about what happened. I need her to know that I know what went on. I don't think she deliberately did any of this. I think she was incompetent and inexperi-

enced and she was scared of the fact that she became emotionally, if not romantically, involved with me. I feel like a meeting with her would be better than what I've gotten so far.

Before confronting the professional, clients have to assess their readiness to make such a vital move. If this action comes not from their core self but rather from an allegiance to an internal or external "should" or sense of duty, clients come away feeling hollow and incomplete. A client described her sense of futility after rotely writing a letter to her physician:

> I had trouble when I was writing the letter. It didn't describe what the violation was really like. It seemed kind of jargony. I kept thinking that it sounded really stupid and it didn't have much of an impact. And I kept picturing that his nurse was going to read it first anyway.

If clients are not <u>internally solid</u> about what they need to do for themselves, they run the risk of leaving themselves out of the process. If they proceed before they are ready, they run the risk of being derailed by the professional. Lacking a store of inner knowledge to draw from for protection, clients are prone to attend more to the professional's reactions and needs rather than to their own. If this happens, clients are revictimized in that they fall prey once again to the role reversal that was so damaging in the first place.

On confronting her therapist, a client described how she fell into caretaking the professional because she had not yet done the work that would allow her to stay focused on herself. Unbeknown to the client, who was in therapy because of an extramarital affair, her therapist was also seeing her lover at the same time when and at the same clinic where another therapist was seeing her husband. The client discovered the arrangement when she ran into her lover in the parking lot of the clinic:

I called the therapist and told her that I needed to talk on a personal level and discuss what had happened. She told me that she was relieved but scared. When I went to see her, I told her that she had hurt me by seeing this man with whom I was having the affair. She said she was sorry about the decision, that she had talked to colleagues and realized her mistake. Since she had stopped seeing this man as a client, she said she was hurt that I had decided not to continue therapy with her. Then she started crying. I thought, "Now I realize what it's like to be a therapist because here is this person in shambles and crying." I felt sorry for her. Everything I said she turned on herself. Everything was about her. I guess when I think about it now, I really didn't get to say anything without her focusing the conversation on herself. And I played into it! I really didn't get much from her because she made herself so little. I would have liked to talk to her a little longer, but she ended the session prematurely. She left the room crying. She couldn't take it anymore.

Before meeting with the professional, clients have to be clear about their expectations. While the encounter is an opportunity for mutual honesty and relational healing, the goal for clients is to center on what they must do for themselves, not on a specific outcome that is based on the professional's response. If clients base their success on what they get from the professional or look to the professional for acknowledgment and validation, they give away their own power to make themselves and their perceptions of events credible. They turn the measuring rod over to the professional. Therefore, clients have to recognize that they can proceed and accomplish their purpose even if the professional does not respond well or participate fully in the process.

A client described how she confronted her minister after he sexually abused her. While his response was clearly pathological, the client felt accomplished because of how beautifully she attended to herself to avoid being further victimized by his behavior:

I made an appointment to see him. I went by myself, which was very foolish, but I'm really glad I did it. He was soft-spoken and nice to me. He said that he knew he would see me again but that he hadn't known when it would be. I told him that after our meeting, I would be done with him. I told him how angry I was. I told him I had been in the hospital because I wanted to kill him and then myself. He looked real taken aback. We talked for a while, and then he said, "I'm really sorry." I needed and wanted to hear that.

But he also did some real creepy stuff. He told me he still loved me and that the only way I could really recover was to trust him again. I told him that I wanted no relationship with him. I asked him if he told battered women to go home and live with their husbands and trust them again. I could feel his charisma and I thought, "This is nuts. This guy is nuts. I don't need all this." When I left, I told him I was through with him. I made some comment about sending him my therapy bills for what he had done to me. He looked at me and said, "You're not done with me. You're still angry." I just said, "I'm done." And I walked out.

I went to the park and cried. I realized he didn't mean his apology. I also saw how sick and dangerous he is and how it was not me. I also saw that he is not this giant monster who is in charge but a human being who makes horrendous mistakes. He is this very sad, very dangerous person who is hurting people and who had hurt me a lot. The biggest part for me is that I'm through the shame. I don't feel the need to be protected like I was in the hospital because I know I'm not crazy. I feel healthier than I've ever been and better than I ever have in my entire life.

For their encounter with the professional to be healing, clients have to bear witness to their experience by telling their story from their core self. By doing so, they silence the inner censor that assesses the accuracy of the description, evaluates what is appropriate and what is not, and judges the rightness or wrongness of their behavior and their feelings. Making their reality their truth means letting it stand just as it is.

As clients feel the satisfaction that comes from honoring their own needs in the presence of the professional, not having betrayed or compromised their truth during the conversation, and having been respectful toward themselves and the professional in telling their story, they regain their worth, power, and control. They carry the achievement of having replaced their helplessness with strength, their terror with self-assertion, and their shame with the claim that, like the professional, they are people who deserve to be respected, valued, and treated with consideration. Realizing they came through for themselves establishes the safety they initially tried to create by being hypervigilant and avoiding fear-provoking situations. The knowledge that they did what they needed to do for themselves during the confrontation gives them the sense of control they tried to gain by inappropriately accepting the responsibility for the violation.

HEALING THE RELATIONSHIP:
THE PROFESSIONAL'S TASK

Just as victimized clients have to commit to taking risks on their own behalf, so too do professionals have to decide whether to face what they did. Often the realization that they made a mistake surfaces only after they are hurt by its consequences or when they are confronted by the client. Regardless of how professionals first come to recognize their errors, their reaction is identical: They want desperately to make the problem disappear. Once they see that this will not happen, they begin to experience their own powerlessness. Indeed, the fact that something they did is now out of their control leaves professionals feeling helpless, vulnerable, and frightened—as if they are as much a victim as the client. Once the violation is out in the open, professionals feel caught between their need for safety and their need for resolution. Yet, like the client, they have to choose between living in their fear or taking additional risks. Unfortunately, neither decision frees them from feeling endangered. Their anxiety is a constant with which they have to live while they face their existential dilemmas and uncertain choices.

Feeling the Shock, Shame, and Terror

Most professionals are not consciously aware that they have committed a violation. (See section titled "A Warning about Character-Disordered Professionals and Clients" in Chapter VII for a discussion of character-disordered professionals.) Having already cancelled out reality by denying the significance of the relationship, the power differential, or the truth about their needs, they are surprised and overwhelmed when that reality suddenly emerges and they learn that they did something inappropriate or wrong. Many professionals may be stunned by the fact that they have never considered the impact of their seemingly innocent behavior on clients. Others may be horrified by the fact that they ignored their initial apprehension about something they did and now feel the full weight of their act. Having glimpsed the overwhelming implications, most professionals go into shock to defend against the self-condemnation that inevitably follows.

Indeed, nothing is more excruciatingly painful than the shame professionals feel about having done something wrong. A therapist described how she experienced her loss of self-worth:

> We're all supposed to know what is right and what is wrong. If you don't, you wonder what's the matter with you. Because I made this mistake, I felt like I did not measure up, like maybe I came from bad people. It was more than just feeling stupid. It was sort of like coming from bad stock.

This deep sense of imperfection is difficult to tolerate, for professionals expect themselves to be people of honor, quality, and superior character. When they cannot live up to these ideals, they feel ashamed because who they pretend to be is not, in fact, who they are. An attorney who specializes in professional malpractice expressed it this way:

> The shame many professionals feel is disabling and even life-threatening. They have fallen from such a high view of themselves to such a low state. When they go that way, they see only blackness. But like every other human being they are fallible. They make mistakes. I tell my clients, "The reason you feel so bad about yourself is that you thought too much of yourself. You thought you could not make mistakes, that you could not get yourself into this kind of bind. But, as a matter of fact, you are no different from anyone else." Realizing that they are like other human beings can be a very depressing experience. Maybe it's the first time they have ever looked fully at themselves.

Professionals also feel terror—the terror of the unknown. Some may be afraid of what they now have to face about themselves. Others may fear what may happen to them professionally. Still others may dread having to face the client. Stripped of exclusive control, professionals feel defenseless. Unable to divine the future or manage the outcome, they feel in danger. A cleric described what he almost did as he tried to predict what lay ahead:

> I fully expected I was going to have to resign. Late one night I found myself in tears as I started to clean out my office. I called a pastor who had been through something similar to my situation. He encouraged me to get professional help. I remember him saying to me, "You're worth it." That was a real affirming thing to hear because I was so down on myself. I had been looking in the want ads for a job as a truck driver. I felt like my career was coming to an end.

Self-Protection versus Self-Examination

Shame and terror compel professionals to seek relief. In striving to bolster their self-esteem and to feel less powerless, they have to make a critical choice: "Will I put my primary energy into protecting myself or into examining and understanding how I allowed the violation to occur?"

Those who take the first path are solely concerned with protecting themselves. Thus, they work hard to repress or minimize their shame by excusing what they did: "It's no big deal. There were extenuating circumstances over which I had no control. Besides, I meant well." These rationalizations are, to some degree, true—clients always feel the violation to be larger than professionals perceive it to be, there are always extenuating circumstances, and most professionals do function out of a core of benevolence. While there are grains of truth in every rationalization, it does not excuse the greater truth. Moreover, objectifying the client and the violation may well shrink the situation to a manageable size. Yet professionals who elect to psychologically distance themselves from the situation also elect to cut themselves off from the route to true self-forgiveness, which is the deeper reality, and curtail the healing of the relationship.

Those who take the second path are also motivated by their drive to ease their intense shame, but rather than protecting themselves, they choose to enter the dark cave within to look for answers that may be enlightening. Indeed, they find it too painful to live imprisoned by their disgrace and emotionally cut off from the human community. Since they know that being haunted by shame, frozen with fear, and internally locked up will diminish their life, they are responsive to what they must do both to heal and to forgive themselves. It is, therefore, their reverence for their own life that compels them to take this alternative path.

To answer the question "How did it happen?" as fully as possible, professionals who have committed a boundary violation have to be honest about what set the stage for the violation. They have to let themselves know what made it easy for them to take advantage of the client. Examples abound: Perhaps a physician was stressed out from a busy week and blew when a demanding and anxious patient asked one more question. Perhaps a cleric was in financial trouble and knew a parishioner who could be trusted to invest his money in high-risk stocks.

Perhaps an attorney who had knee problems consulted a physician who was also a client because her skills were so outstanding. Most of the time, professionals find that their misuse of the client did not grow out of some malicious intent or unresolved psychological issue. Rather, the violation happened because they were unaware of their needs and the client was convenient. Using him or her made their life easier. Within this reality, professionals begin to grasp how they used their greater power in the relationship to cross the boundary and take what they needed from the client.

To make sense out of their behavior, some professionals also have to examine why they crossed the boundary with a particular client. For many professionals, the choice of client is irrelevant, just a matter of who was available at the time. For other professionals, however, a certain client may have held special meaning and awakened vulnerabilities about which they were unaware. A therapist described why she befriended a gay client who had AIDS and encouraged his gift-giving:

> To come to grips with what happened, I had to understand what this client meant to me and why I had tried to get so much from him for myself. I realized that when I was a little kid, I was taught that gay men hate women. Therefore, I had been very afraid when I started working with HIV-infected clients. I worried that I wouldn't be able to do my job well because they wouldn't like me because I was a woman. I think I made this client special, accepted his gifts, and relaxed my rules because I wanted him to like me as much as I liked him. By giving me things, he made me feel accepted.

Discovering what motivated their behavior only partially answers the question "How did it happen?" For a complete accounting, professionals also have to examine how they gave themselves permission to disregard the limits. Perhaps they told themselves that the therapy was over, that their behavior did not interfere with the performance of their medical or legal duties, or that their actions met the standard of conduct for other clerics or teachers. Although there may be many variations on this theme, the sole outcome is that they either minimized the relationship or equalized the power differential. A minister shared how he skewed reality about his role with a parishioner to justify using her to meet his needs:

> Since I was in the process of leaving the parish, I technically wasn't her minister anymore. Therefore, I decided we could be friends. I also felt that I hadn't been appreciated, respected, or treated as I should have been in this particular parish. I didn't deal with my resentment in a healthy way. Instead, I used this woman as a way to get back at the congregation.
>
> Even though I was aware that it was a misuse of power, particularly in light of this woman's vulnerability, I made a convenient legalistic interpretation that I had ceased being the pastor of that parish on such and such a date to satisfy my own self-centered needs. I could rationalize continuing to relate to her because of *her neediness*. I didn't let myself know how much I was taking from her. I thought I was just giving to her. In my own mind, I emphasized her emotional need and my contribution to her while de-emphasizing the self-centered part of it.

By dissecting their faulty logic, professionals begin to see how they selectively structured reality to fit their own agenda. Not only did they deceive themselves about who they are and who they were to the client, but they also refused to acknowledge their needs and the fact that those needs could get in the way of their obligations to the client. Indeed, only when they can remember and appreciate the basic vulnerability of the client, the surrendering of part of his or her life to their safe keeping, and the level of faith that accompanies the client's trust can they see the faultiness of their reasoning. Like the client, professionals have to reassess and modify their deluded logic to let in the truth about the violation and who was responsible for it.

Since denial is a self-protective defense against that which is unaccept-
able, those professionals who elect to take off their mask have to envi-
sion some greater benefit to risk such private and public exposure.
Usually, it is the unrelenting pressure from their shame and their intense
need for internal resolution that push them to engage in such rigorous
self-scrutinization. The drive to restore their own life and self-respect and
to live peacefully with themselves helps them to undertake tasks that
would otherwise be impossible. In answering what he would tell other
professionals, a rabbi who had abused a parishioner said:

> In a nutshell, it would be "Physician, heal thyself." I needed to
> heal my own self to maximize my effectiveness as a rabbi. I was
> certified on paper to do ministry when I wasn't ready to. Now I
> know that the most effective rabbis are the ones who have achieved
> a certain level of healing or growth in their own person.

Self-Protection versus Acknowledgment

As professionals make sense out of their own behavior, their deeper
responsibility to the covenant begins to surface. While facing the truth
of their mistake leaves them humbled and more accepting of their
human imperfections, it also leaves them with an existential guilt that, in
the words of Martin Buber, "occurs when someone injures an order of
the human world whose foundations he knows and recognizes as those
of his own existence and of all common human existence" (1988, p.
117).

The guilt for having diminished life compels professionals to take
corrective action. Yet, they hold back. Afraid for their own well-being,
they again find themselves at a critical juncture and in conflict about
whether to defend themselves or to repair the damage with the client.

Today, this struggle is not just a theoretical debate. Clients increasingly turn to those who hold even greater power to punish professionals
who commit violations. The surge in lawsuits, the increase in com-

plaints to superiors, and the more widespread use of regulatory boards by the public to express grievances make negative consequences for professionals a more likely possibility than ever before. Acknowledging the mistake with a client, therefore, could well be dangerous because it might be viewed legally as an admission of guilt. With this tool, a client who wants to get even or is susceptible to outside direction might take action that could endanger the career and livelihood of the professional with whom he or she was involved.

Such a threat makes it difficult for professionals to ascertain reality. Since the shame they feel about what they did and the terror of possibly exposing it to the client and/or others make them paranoid, professionals cannot tell if their apprehension is a accurate response to the peril that is real in the outside world or is a result of what they feel inside.

Whether or not their paranoia is realistic and factually based, it can poison their view of the wider community and how they feel about themselves. Seen through this filter, everyone is a potential enemy, any mistake is tantamount to a sin, and the outside world appears dangerous. As a result, professionals may retreat within to live in the fear that they believe will protect them from possible harm. Like the client who shuts down and avoids professionals to stay safe, they constrict who they are. By cutting themselves off from the fullness of life and curtailing the freedom of their movement, they create an internal jailor who admonishes and punishes them as deeply and as harshly as any public sanction they might otherwise receive.

An attorney who has represented many professionals described the severity of this seemingly no-win decision and the long-term consequences for those who choose the route of self-protection:

> The decision about direction is so personal in their future that it would be presumptuous and extreme for anyone else to make that decision for them. Yet, I don't think any of the professionals I've worked with get any peace until they confront reality. I think that

to the degree that they can slip past the system and not deal with reality, they will be sick. The best outcomes I've seen are the direct result of confrontation, truthfulness, and an acceptance of reality. That's easy to say. It's difficult to do.

The bind for professionals, therefore, is nearly impossible. If they decide to give to the client, they potentially hurt themselves. If they decide not to act or respond, they turn their back on the truth as they now know it to be, thereby compromising the values on which they base their lives.

For most professionals, the decision to acknowledge the violation grows out of the belief that reconciling with the client will provide the avenue for alleviating their shame. To "go public," however, professionals have to surrender a part of themselves. To let go of striving for perfection or trying to manage the outcome themselves, they have to place their safety in the hands of something larger. Some put their faith in a higher power. Some lean on the knowledge that they are doing the "right thing." Some decide to trust the guidance from a colleague or supervisor. Uniting with something larger than themselves helps them let go of control and turn over their shame.

Their decision to hold themselves accountable to the client and to the original intent of the relationship begins the resolution. While each professional has to decide what must be done to correct the wrong, fully acknowledging the violation may mean that professionals need to put themselves through the experience of hearing the client's story. Although this ordeal is extremely painful, professionals' willingness to reexperience and bear witness to the violation from the client's perspective transfers the pain to the responsible party. This telling is also a gift to professionals in that they have the opportunity to learn firsthand the significance of who they were in the eyes of another. The remorse and sorrow which professionals commonly experience allow the client to feel accepted and validated. Letting the client have an impact on how they see themselves also mends the client's experience of having been diminished. As each accepts what the other gives, they reexperience their connectedness and repair the violation that tore them apart. Making their paths one is the healing needed by both.

A therapist described what both she and her client went through as the client was helped to fully appreciate and share her situation and the therapist forced herself to absorb the gravity of her seemingly innocuous mistake.

One of my clients, herself a therapist, attended a psychology conference led by a national figure in my field. Since the conference had been my idea, I felt responsible for the day and for handling the arrangements for lunch. I felt a lot of pressure to make the experience enjoyable for the presenter. At the last minute, I found I could not take her to lunch myself. With little forethought, I asked some of the attendees to join her instead. One of the people I approached was my client.

Even though I was trading on our relationship, I blocked my awareness of this fact and did not give her position as my client top priority. Instead, I, as the conference arranger, believed that I had approached her as an attendee who had much in common with this national expert. I was so preoccupied with the luncheon arrangements that I overlooked the fact that my client was considering moving to the city where the presenter lived. When I asked her, she immediately agreed to go to lunch and I relaxed, reassured that the expert was in good hands.

I did not realize what I had done until a colleague shared a story that same week about how she had used a client. I still remember the searing pangs of shame and guilt as I recognized what I had done and what I now had to face.

At our next session, the client said, "Words can't express how appreciative I am that you asked me to go to lunch with the presenter. Whether this is what you meant or not, I felt like you were telling me that I was an adult and that I was ready to move to this new city."

I remember my sinking feeling as I realized what had happened. I had totally minimized my importance, the extent of the transference, and the meaning that she, as my client, would have inferred from my request. "Well," I said, "I've got a lot of talking to do with you. There is something very important that we have to deal with. You need to know that what happened at the conference was inappropriate."

"What do you mean?" she asked.

"There was a violation of you," I said. "I asked you to go to lunch because of your position in the community. I placed my need to put good people together ahead of the fact that you are my client."

My client looked as if she had been slapped. Appalled by what I had done, she looked at me in shock and said, "My God, that really was one." After a few moments of silence, she said, "I feel so robbed. When you asked me to go to lunch, I felt really cared about by you in what I thought was a clean way. It was so special and I was flying high. Now I see that that's not what it was at all."

"Yes," I admitted, "you were responding to the lunch situation out of the context of being a client. You knew that and I neglected that."

The size of my betrayal of this client became more evident when I insisted she honor her anger in our following session. I had violated her trust and placed her therapy in jeopardy by what I did. I knew that we could not even assess whether or not to continue her work until we had dealt fully and honestly with what had happened.

She began by saying, "When you first told me it was a violation, I felt robbed and I felt real hurt. I also put it all on me, believing something was wrong with me for my fantasy about my specialness. I told myself that you were honest and said it was a violation. How many people would be that honest? How many people would care? But that kept me away from my anger.

"When I realized what this all really meant to me, I got furious. You see, I had made up this story to myself. My mother doesn't want me to move to this city because she says it's too dangerous. Whenever I experience my mother's caring for me, it turns out it's about what she needs. I know she wants me to take care of her and not to move away. When you asked me to have lunch with this expert, I felt you were giving me a clear message and your blessing to move. I felt like you were turning me over to your own parent, to someone you admired. I decided you were not like my mother. I felt released because I realized you did not need me in the way she does. She will never let go. So what you did made me feel crazy because I had this very nice, wonderful fantasy that wasn't true at all. In fact, your putting your needs first was just what my mother does or very similar.

"I have looked to you to set boundaries. So I'm disappointed and angry that you violated them. Your being insensitive doesn't feel like you. I'm just having a hell of a time figuring out why. Maybe some of your own issues with me were in there."

"I don't think so," I said.

"So I wasn't even in there at all?" my client asked.

"Right," I said. "I almost wish I could say that you had something to do with this because it would give me some way out. I think it happened principally because of my relationship with this presenter. I disregarded everything else and did what was most convenient and easiest for myself at the time."

Processing this experience with my client went on for some time. Later in our discussion, my client said, "You look sad."

"I do feel bad," I said, "but I don't want to change the focus to dissipate your anger. It's right on and I'm pleased that you have it."

"Well," my client said, "part of my anger was that you aren't perfect. Now that I see you in pain I realize you can't be perfect. If you were, you wouldn't have any feelings."

"I do feel bad about it," I said. "I left myself by compromising my own values, I left our relationship, and I absolutely left you. I'll never forget your words when I told you what had happened and how you looked as you dropped from the high you had felt into the hell that suddenly appeared."

"That's what made me so furious," my client said. "How could YOU make a mistake?"

"I do expect myself to be perfect," I said. "Maybe it's good for me to be forced to look at the fact that I am human."

"One thing I've learned from this," said my client, "is that I really do have to learn to watch out for myself. I can't turn myself over to you as some superhuman god. It has made a big difference knowing that I have to deal with this in our relationship and that I better take care of myself."

The resolution of the violation and reconciliation is both sorrowful and healing. As the myth of perfection dies and is replaced by a deeper appreciation of the client's vulnerability and the professional's proclivities, both parties grieve over what now is forever a part of their history. Paradoxically, going through this process together restores the connection and creates a closer bond that comes from the genuine presentation and acceptance of who each is to the other.

While the roles of the professional and the client are not the same, the violation explodes the world for both of them and sends them on a similar journey. Like the client, professionals strive to gain clarity to make sense out of what went wrong. They, too, search for safety to reduce their fear and for control to lessen their helpless. Like the client, they need support to relieve their shame and isolation. Unlike the client, who internalizes the violation, professionals are not engaged in self-defeating behavior when they pursue the goals of clarity, safety, control, and validation. Indeed, achieving these goals not only helps professionals but gives the client the tools he or she needs to move on. The client gains clarity when professionals give information that makes order out of what happened. The client gains safety when professionals no longer avoid exploring the truth about themselves and assume responsibility for who they are. The client gains more control when professionals rebalance the relationship by acknowledging the wrong and holding themselves accountable. The client gains the validation that releases him or her from the violation when professionals face their shame and accept the consequences of their behavior.

For professionals, this process is an act of atonement by which they seek to right what was wronged. It also allows them to feel worthwhile again. The decision to embark on this journey ultimately rests on whether they have faith enough to enter the unknown and can trust something larger than themselves. If they can take this step, they become a catalyst in that the client is encouraged to reestablish his or her trust to risk as well. While nothing can change the fact of the violation, the meaning it holds for both client and professional can be significantly altered by this process.

REBUILDING THE CLIENT'S TRUST

No one of us can survive alone. Our capacity to trust, therefore, is precious because without it we are isolated from the human community. Unfortunately, this capacity is reduced whenever a professional violates the relationship with a client. For victimized clients, opening themselves to trust again is a slow and gradual process, for the evidence against it is often more substantial than the logic that supports it. Often clients feel as if they are plunging into deep water over and over again. To make it safe for them, professionals have to establish a well-demarcated relationship that is predictable and caring.

Risking Again: The Client's Task

To risk their trust, clients have to diminish the hold of the violation on their core self. They have to convert it from an injury that disables them into an experience that moves them forward. This transformation cannot be forced, however. It happens when clients are ready to restore their faith and are open to whatever the future holds.

To venture out, though, clients have to give themselves something secure on which to lean, something that speaks to and resolves the internal discord caused by their terror, a belief that sustains them as they encounter the unknown. Most clients give birth to this belief out of the ashes of their pain. With it, they can assign a new meaning to the injury. A client described how she resolved her struggle to move out from under her helplessness: "I realized that the pain I was in had a larger purpose. I needed to heal my insecurity and self-doubt. I had to step out of shoes of fear and move into shoes of confidence."

The ability of clients to transform the violation and infuse it with life-affirming potential is a tribute to the healing power that resides within us all. Their connection to their new truth releases clients from the bondage of the past. It gives clients a way to trust that something meaningful can emerge from something hurtful. It gives them strength. In this transformation, clients re-birth their optimism and the possibility of again placing their faith in what lies beyond their power to know. Using the analogy of removing a piece of glass from her thumb, a client described releasing herself from her imprisonment:

> While washing dishes, I cut my thumb with a drinking glass that had broken under water. It took eight stitches to close the wound. Then came the pain, fierce and sleep-disturbing. Then healing. A year passed.
>
> One day while riding a bus home from work, I noticed a white pimple on the surface of my crooked scar. It was painful. I picked at it gently. It broke open and out came a piece of glass. Sharp and clean, it came out in a tiny bubble of white fluid. I got a sick feeling as the glass emerged, thinking how long this sharpness had been in my body. I looked at it for a long time. Then I took a tissue from my purse and wrapped the sliver in it. I felt release when I threw it away. I wondered at how the glass could have

stayed in my thumb that long without my knowing it, a piercing reminder of how deep the cut had been and how the cutting hadn't finished for a long, long time.

As the wound of the violation begins to heal, clients seek to rejoin the larger community. However, they enter it differently from how they had before. Less naive about what can happen, they promise themselves not to compromise who they are and what they need. They also vow to honor their wariness and take seriously their skepticism. They know it is important not to give themselves away. Indeed, their ability to follow through on these commitments ensures their future safety.

Paradoxically, the more clients can trust themselves, the more open they are with professionals. Balancing between their wariness and their accessibility, they learn that trusting does not mean surrendering who they are or ridding themselves of their apprehensiveness. Rather, trusting is about bringing all of who they are into the relationship. Their rapprochement must, therefore, be slow. Not only must they monitor the professional's behavior, but they also must test whether or not they can trust themselves to act on their own behalf. A client described his cautiousness and how he verified his control over the process by holding himself back from being totally available to his therapist:

It took me a long time to trust. I didn't feel like I was going to get hurt, but I just didn't feel trusting. Even though I felt like it was okay with her, I still wasn't going to give that piece over. The last month or two, I've felt really warm toward her. I've felt really good since then.

Another client described how she gained confidence in her ability to keep herself safe by monitoring her physician's behavior and using her internal responses to guide her:

I'm a total fiend when I go to the doctor now. I ask, "What are you going to do?" "Why are you doing that?" The doctor I see now is okay because she cares about my pain. Others I saw acted like I was making it up. But she gave me a sense that something could be done. In that way, she gave me back some confidence.

Both of these clients honored what they needed before they gave their trust. Their openness emerged out of learning that they could rely on their own judgment.

Providing a Corrective Experience:
The Professional's Task

Boundary violations are disorders of disconnection. Since recovery is a process of reconnecting, professionals have to create the opportunity for a safe attachment. Whether the rebuilding of the client's trust is done with the help of the professional who committed the violation or a new one, establishing a respectful environment does not require specialized skills or knowledge. Rather, it calls for professionals to maintain the covenant that binds them first to the care of the person being represented, treated, taught, or ministered to, and second to working within the context of hallowed and transcendent principles. To ensure the success of the corrective experience, professionals must (1) take charge of the relationship, (2) accept responsibility for having greater power than the client, and (3) consistently place the client's needs first. The reemergence of the client's willingness to trust is a natural bonus that obtains when professionals make an authentic connection and establish their professional reliability over time.

To take charge of the relationship, professionals have to be willing to accept their greater authority and use it to guide the client through the unknown. Frequently, professionals must structure the client's role and teach him or her what to expect of the relationship. They may have to place limits on the interaction so that they and the client can accomplish their joint purpose. For example, an attorney may need to restrict the amount of telephone contact that he or she will have with a needy client so as not to foster an unhealthy dependency. Similarly, a teacher at a small liberal arts college shared her decision about using students to babysit:

> I made a mental rule for myself that I would never use someone who was currently in a class with me as a babysitter. I tell my students that once they start as a babysitter, they can never take a class with me again. That's all a part of the student-teacher relationship. How could I give a *C* to a student who had just changed my daughter's dirty diaper? I have had to keep these lines clear so that I can function as a teacher and be fair to my students.

Given such limits, the client knows the parameters of the relationship and can predict, at least to some extent, how the professional will respond should the client cross over the line of what is appropriate or in his or her best interests. Moreover, he or she can be confident that the professional will act to redraw the boundary. A client described how a therapist handled her wish to be special and how it affected her trust:

> After a therapist abused me, it took me a long time before I saw one I could really trust. One of the consequences that came clear to me was how incredibly special the boundary violation had made me feel. I was surprised to find myself pushing to be special with this new therapist. I would ask her to hold my hand or give me a hug. I'm a weaver and I would bring in my craftwork to get her reaction.
>
> Instead of just responding to my requests, she had me process out loud what I really wanted from her and why. I realized the kind of grandiosity I was operating under and the secondary gain I had gotten from my inappropriate relationship with the previous therapist and was now trying to get again. She didn't leave a stone unturned. It was very helpful for me to have that mirror held up.

To accept responsibility for their greater power, professionals have to submerge their own needs and discipline themselves to use their power within the constraints of the relationship. Since the sole purpose of the relationship is to meet the client's needs, screening professional decisions through the filter of the ethos of care helps establish a security system to protect against acts that might otherwise rupture the bond. Being accountable to the relationship is an exacting process. Making it preeminent means developing a subservient posture for professional purposes so as to be constantly mindful and responsive to the nuances in the interaction. Being so observant requires tremendous concentration and awareness. A lesbian therapist who was "out" in the community described her submission to doing whatever was necessary to protect the integrity of the relationship. Because she made her connection with the client her ultimate priority, she ensured her safety:

> I left my car at a service station early in the morning to be repaired. Thinking I had a ride to pick it up, I found out at the end of the day that I didn't. Feeling stranded, I asked my late-afternoon client to give me a ride to the station. It was the most uncomfortable ride I've ever taken. Then I made a second bad decision. I decided to ignore my reaction and not to talk about it with my client. Five years later, when she returned for more therapy, I began to appreciate the significance of my original decisions.
>
> In one of our sessions, the client began talking about how she had been sexually abused as an adolescent by her youth minister. He had taken her for a ride in his new car way out in the country. During the entire ride, the client had been terrified that she'd be raped. I remember thinking, "Oh God, I hope she doesn't bring up my having asked her to give me a ride. I don't want to deal with it." Gradually, though, I realized that *I* had to bring it up. Not talking about it would be an additional violation because I would be giving her the message that somehow it was okay for me to have crossed the boundary but not okay for the minister.
>
> I decided to broach the subject with her and asked, "Do you remember the time I asked you to give me a ride?" The client said she did but that she didn't want to talk about it. She was angry that I had brought it up and actively tried to diminish the importance of what had happened between us. Finally, I suggested she see a therapist who could help her confront me. Only then did the

client begin to feel how important she was and to know how important our professional connection with each other was to me.

To place the client's needs first, professionals have to bestow their reverence for life onto the client and use their own life-sustaining energy to respond to what is needed. To accord such sanctity to the client's condition, professionals first have to respect their own needs and gather the energy to give by getting what they need for themselves outside the relationship. In honoring their own needs, they pay homage and attest to the basic human condition. They also legitimize, through their repetitive tending, the necessity of responding to the unequivocal nature of their own hunger.

Honoring what is needed to sustain and enhance life for themselves helps professionals transfer that regard to the client. The value professionals place on the needs of the client also elevates and validates the client's right to pursue them. This is essential because the client who has been hurt may question or even hide his or her needs. Fearful that he or she caused the violation, the client may feel ashamed whenever he or she feels vulnerable. By educating the client to accept and value his or her needs, professionals help remove the stigma of the violation. By intensifying the client's belief in the validity of his or her situation and demonstrating that a professional's job is to attend to what is necessary, professionals also empower the client and strengthen his or her resolve to take good care of himself or herself. A client described how her new physician reacted to her needs and how his spontaneous behavior helped remove her shame and bolster her self-confidence and trust:

It took a whole year before I could tell my new doctor what had happened before. I remember telling him, "My previous physician used to tell me that my physical problems were due to not dating." This doctor was shocked. Because of his reaction and the fact that he had found I was suffering from chronic mononucleosis, I realized my previous physician had made a wrong diagnosis. Because of my new doctor's dismay, he made it clear that a medical condition does not grow out of that fact that one doesn't date. It felt wonderful to get his reaction. I've just not had this kind of luck in finding a doctor before.

Giving the client a corrective experience redraws the boundary that guards the space between the client's vulnerability and the professional's power. Consistently taking charge of the relationship provides the client with safety. Assuming responsibility for holding greater power by being accountable to the relationship injects humility into the connection. Vaccinating the relationship with this medicine opens the way for the professional's care and curbs the possible distancing that can highlight the professional's "superiority" and, in comparison, the client's lesser status. Finally, placing the client's needs first restores the client's visibility and lessens the sense of diminishment caused by the violation.

Healing the relationship cannot avoid being a painful undertaking for both clients and professionals. As they get in touch with their anger, clients naturally gravitate toward seeking revenge. As they get in touch with their shame and terror, professionals naturally gravitate toward protecting themselves. Taking these respective paths leaves both groups bound to the injury and unfinished with each other. Deciding to heal the wound requires clients and professionals to take a different path. They have to move beyond an intellectual understanding and instead reach out to each other to heal the pain each feels. Righting what was wronged necessitates a deep commitment to self and to rebalancing the ledger of obligations that define the professional-client relationship. Placing their faith in what is life-affirming allows both professionals and clients to risk themselves and make this journey.

VII

BARRIERS TO RELATIONAL HEALING

A S PROFESSIONALS, WE HAVE a moral and ethical obligation to heal the client and the relationship we have injured. Indeed, not to address the violation is another violation, in that we again nullify the client's needs. Relational healing, however, is unlikely to be the option of choice because of the many barriers that stand in our way.

Clearly, there is little professional encouragement to mend the damaged connection. Instead of promulgating a relational model, our colleagues and educational and professional institutions exhort us to take a self-protective stance, as does the culture at large, which increasingly promotes an adversarial model of justice for righting wrongs. Against this backdrop, relational healing appears unwise and naive, even foolhardy.

The current climate does not support such attempts and neither do we. The personal barriers we encounter in ourselves, the structural deterrents that block our way, and the societal norms that skew our moral vision make it practically impossible for us to proceed. We also find new obstacles as we realize we must be wary of the danger posed by professionals and clients who are impaired by a character disorder. Most disturbing and sobering, however, is the realization that our cynicism, pessimism, and mistrust keep us away from relational healing and from using the tools that might work.

PERSONAL BARRIERS

Relational healing is perilous not so much because we fear our clients but because we dread what we may encounter if we look inside ourselves. Most of us measure our work performance against an ideal model. We have one set of standards for ourselves and another set for everyone else. Anointed with power and placed on a pedestal by our society, we easily fall prey to the unrealistic expectation that we *should* be able to transcend our own needs and human frailties.

Because we base our self-esteem on our ability to meet these superhuman demands, any mistake can be devastating to our basic but precarious sense of worth. To save ourselves from the shame of our mortalness, we distort reality. We reason that since the client made the problem visible, he or she is responsible for the pain we feel. This faulty logic leads us to fight the client instead of confronting the monster of perfectionism that lies within.

Moreover, if we admit that the violation derives from our own unmet needs, we may have to disrupt our lives in major ways to honor them. For example, a physician plagued by financial concerns may have to cut the number of hours she works and thus the amount of money she makes to ensure her patients' safety. A shy, lonely teacher may have to challenge his primary dependency on students for his social life. An attorney who drinks to drown his feelings of inadequacy may have to risk his reputation and interrupt his practice to enter treatment for chemical dependency.

Even though such changes may be healthy, we resent that we have to make sacrifices if we are to gain for ourselves and our clients. And the truth is, none of us wants to give up something we have earned through hard work and thus feel we are entitled to have. As a result, we opt to deny the violation or place the blame for it elsewhere. To do otherwise seems too costly both emotionally and financially.

STRUCTURAL BARRIERS

During our training to become professionals, we are force-fed certain tenets and attitudes that foster our denial of our needs, who we are, and the importance of the professional-client relationship. Not only are they the basis for and perpetuators of boundary violations, but they also are antithetical to relational healing. We are placed at risk, therefore, not just by our personal shortcomings but also by the professions in which we practice.

Medicine

The charge to physicians is to sustain life. In light of this mandate, medical training is of necessity rigorous. Coping with the psychological, mental, and physical stresses heaped on students is considered an essential rite of passage to becoming a bona fide physician. These inordinately high professional demands not only normalize and glorify physicians' suffering but also feed their perfectionism and breed a grandiose self-image. As one physician said of himself and his colleagues, "We develop a bond because we go through some tough experiences together that the rest of the world doesn't have. Since you put in that kind of effort and pay those kind of dues, you come out thinking you're pretty special and are owed something for your suffering."

At its worst, medical training is abusive. Indeed, the answers to published and unpublished surveys of 1,200 medical students attending twelve different schools demonstrate that students are subjected to verbal, psychological, and even physical abuse from their superiors (Sheehan, Sheehan, White, Leibowitz, & Baldwin, 1990; Steinbrook, 1990). According to Dr. DeWitt Baldwin, Jr., director of the American Medical Association's division of medical education research, physicians who have been "treated in this manner may well carry over those attitudes and behaviors to their patients and students" (Steinbrook, 1990, p. 29A).

Denied permission to a large extent to have human frailties and therefore to be real, physicians have but one recourse: They distance themselves from the pressure by objectifying their patients. This distance is a psychological shield, however, that also blocks physicians from picking up the cues in the relationship that help monitor how they use their power. As a result, physicians are apt to disregard the vulnerability of their patients as well as their impact on them and shun the personal demands inherent in relational healing.

The current thrust toward expediency reflected by the burgeoning of large and impersonal health-care systems in this country increases the likelihood that physicians will be even less accessible to patients in the future and even less accountable for the treatment they deliver or fail to deliver. This trend can only exacerbate the practice of objectifying the patient and discounting the relationship.

Education

The charge to teachers is to pursue and impart knowledge and engender creativity. These pursuits are embodied in the concept "academic freedom," which is the sine qua non of higher education. Academic freedom is revered as essential to the process of open inquiry. In practice, it gives educators a great deal of autonomy. Beyond their classroom commitments, they can set their own hours, follow their own research interests, use their own methods to teach subject matter, and make performance demands on students without outside interference. This highly prized freedom is, however, a double-edged sword because of the vacuum in which teachers operate—a vacuum with few restrictions on how they use their power, few guidelines about their interactions with students, and little reaction from the outside when they overstep relational boundaries. Academic freedom, therefore, can be used as a license to indulge in or as a defense to conceal misbehavior.

While the virtues of autonomy may be publically extolled, many professors feel deeply the weight of their isolation. They are separated from their colleagues by the struggle for power within and between academic departments, the publish-or-perish mentality, and the cutthroat competition for promotions, tenure, and the procuring of grants. The solitariness of their existence along with their removal from "being in the world" leaves them personally needy and responsive to the safety and solace they may feel only with their students.

Left alone and without limits, teachers are therefore prone to make their own rules according to their own advantage. Even without intent, the nonaccountability fostered by the principle of academic freedom becomes a part of and is normalized within the academic environment. Moreover, when problems do occur, the norm of noninterference limits the help that might otherwise be available, deprives teachers of the opportunity to rid themselves of their shame, and, in effect, promotes the secrecy that attends boundary violations.

In some settings, the norms even drive teachers toward being inappropriate with their students. For example, enmeshed boundaries, fluid roles, and impersonal relationships with a singular emphasis on the intellect may be accepted as inherent conditions of academia, even though they are common precursors to boundary violations. Likewise, teachers may step over the line if they are expected to function as surrogate parents or to invite students to live with them or work for them in some capacity outside the classroom. Teachers who do not conform are criticized for being noncollegial.

Their isolation makes teachers vulnerable to using their students, making their own rules, and following without question the normative patterns prescribed by the institution. It also furnishes them with the context for excusing their behavior. Since every academic community is different and tends to establish its own culture, it is easy to justify or explain what happened as perhaps atypical in the "real" world but common in academia or in a particular school. Even though this reasoning distinguishes teachers and the academic community as special and unique, it sets them apart as legitimate outlaws and glorifies the hazards inherent in their isolation. The danger intrinsic in such nonaccountability surfaces again as teachers use the extenuating circumstances of their environment to rationalize their behavior and depreciate the significance of the violation.

Therapy

The charge to therapists is to relate intimately to clients without revealing and interjecting who they are themselves. In their education, therapists therefore are carefully disciplined to curb any demeaning judgments or personal reactions that might jeopardize clients' trust. Instead, they are trained to show only those parts of themselves that are therapeutically significant to their clients' growth. Through this necessary suppression of feelings, therapists in effect cut themselves off from who they really are. Purposefully invisible to their clients, they also risk becoming invisible to themselves.

As they shut down their personhood in the name of professional excellence, they banish what is going on within themselves. For many, their ability to be aware of their personal needs vanishes too. This denial makes them vulnerable to overstepping the relational boundary with clients.

Therapists, by making themselves less, also create a void in the relationship with clients. This space is filled in with the world according to the client's perspective. As the therapist gains a greater understanding of what life is like for the client, a deep intimacy grows between them. As the client becomes more dependent on the therapist's wisdom and presence, the therapist becomes more special and unique in the client's eyes. This specialness feeds the self-esteem of therapists, many of whom forget that the client's projections of who they are grow out of a carefully constructed vacuum of professional nonbeing. These susceptible professionals in effect become dependent on what they personally get from the client. Moreover, if they buy into the client's reality and build their self-image from their client's depiction, they set themselves up to be grandiose and to view any of their human limitations as shameful.

The invisibility of therapists' needs and the environment of intimacy created for clients' growth tend, therefore, to cultivate an unreal world that colludes to block therapists' ability to see what is really happening. They, too, easily loose perspective and respond to their own suppressed needs and the intimacy that surrounds their interaction with the client rather than solely to what the client needs.

To assist them to interrupt their isolation and make them visible to themselves, therapists need ongoing supervision and consultation. Unfortunately, the very training that cultivates their invisibility also establishes the norm that outside assistance is necessary for students and beginners but unnecessary and perhaps inappropriate for experienced and mature therapists. With this normalized attitude, therapists come to believe that the need for help is a sign of immaturity or an admission that perhaps they have done something wrong. The built-in shame about needing then hinders therapists from taking advantage of checks and balances that can keep them out of trouble.

Law

While law is ideally concerned with justice, the real charge to lawyers is to win, to win at any cost. Lawyers learn well through their training to compete aggressively and, if necessary, to bend reality so that they can cognitively move wherever they must to launch a vigorous and successful stratagem. This seemingly utilitarian system breeds, in many cases, amoral technicians who can with clear conscience legitimately be on either side of an issue and legitimately set clients up as potential pawns in a razor-sharp game.

To encourage their relativism and effectiveness, lawyers are taught to sublimate their personal emotions in favor of loftier societal principles and abstractions. While viewing the world through the lens of rationality may simplify and make more manageable a complicated and ambiguous universe, it also enables many lawyers to create an artificial dichotomy by separating their thoughts from their feelings. This division occurs repeatedly over the course of their career. Lawyers readily separate the hard evidence in a case from the subjective, soft and intangible aspects of the situation. They separate legal realities from the emotions of clients. They also insulate themselves from clients' emotionality, giving their primary attention to strategizing their legal position in encounters with their opponent. As a result of this dichotomy, lawyers form a primary relationship not with their clients but with the law. This reality is replicated by the legal system, which ignores for the most part the emotional context of clients' circumstances and makes the dictates of the law the overriding consideration.

For many attorneys the dichotomy between their own thoughts and feelings and the singular focus on rationality impede their ability to respond humanely to themselves and to their clients. By focusing solely on winning regardless of the emotional cost, lawyers are readily susceptible to functioning as automatons who devalue and screen out of their awareness their affective responses except when such responses may be useful manipulative tools in the pursuit of a client's case. Moreover, in their education, lawyers are dissuaded from crediting emotional dimensions of a client's difficulties, particularly if they might jeopardize the outcome desired.

Since they are trained to ignore the interrelationship between thoughts and feelings and to split the world into functional pieces, lawyers are prone to believe that they can use clients for their own needs while remaining available to them in terms of their legal obligations. They apply the same principle of separation when a boundary violation occurs. They argue that since their personal relationship with the client existed outside the context of providing legal services, they should not be held accountable for any behavior that happened beyond the performance of their professional duties.

In many instances, these technically correct arguments allow lawyers to abdicate their responsibility for the emotional aspects of the professional-client encounter and for how their behavior affects the client. Their mistaken contention that they can split who they are from what they do and maintain their objectivity derives from being in a profession that has taught and conditioned them to negate much of who they are.

Religion

The charge to clerics is to be servants of all people. Clerics therefore are taught that they must minister to anyone and place few restrictions on their availability. The immensity of this burden often becomes increasingly overwhelming when clerics learn in seminary that being all things also encompasses developing excellence as an administrator, scholar, orator, liturgist and educator as well as a youth advisor, counselor, and spiritual advisor. As a result of all these expectations, clerics tend to become overresponsible for others at the expense of being underresponsible for themselves.

Since the concept of limits is antithetical to their role, clerics rightfully feel stretched by the demands of their job on the one hand and by the spare permission to attend to their own needs on the other. They are additionally disadvantaged by the egalitarian admonition against doing anything that sets them above and apart from their flock. They therefore deny or work to reduce or hide the power differential inherent in the clergy-parishioner relationship. They believe that having more power than others is presumptuous, an affront to the concept of a shared ministry and a contradiction to the spirit of humbleness before God. Indeed, clerics are indoctrinally restrained from using their authority to set limits with their parishioners while at the same time obligated to remain available, negating their freedom to have and attend to their own needs.

In time, they begin to feel and act like martyrs—special because they are deprived and deprived because they are special. Because they are so self-sacrificing, some clerics feel they are entitled to take from whatever or whoever comes their way as compensation for all they have given. The boundarylessness that permeates their position allows them to easily cross over the line with parishioners. Their denial and diminution of their greater power enable them to escape feeling in charge of the situation.

When boundary violations eventually do occur, clerics are especially hit hard by the reality of their emerging personal needs and the resultant sense of masquerade they have perpetuated with their parishioners. Since denying who they really are is already a normalized way of life, many clerics elect, unfortunately, to hide what happened and to continue to maintain the fraudulent persona prescribed by their role.

The Legacy of Denial

To a greater or lesser extent, the very structure of each of the professions described here creates conditions that increase the likelihood for boundary violations and decrease the possibilities for relational healing. These conditions contribute to the prevailing professional mores that define for us what is normal and valued behavior. What we are taught and what we see modeled by our teachers powerfully influence our perceptions of quality, who we strive to be, and what we strive to do.

Excellence, however, comes with a price tag. Striving for the ideal, we devote ourselves to our art and to perfecting our talents. (Sixty-hour work weeks are common.) To be successful, we cultivate just one dimension of ourselves at the expense of others. Having to be as rational as a lawyer or as selfless as a cleric, for example, would require that we banish all aspects of ourselves that could get in the way. These underdeveloped potentials, however, are exactly what we need to nurture if we are to prevent or heal relational wounds. Lamentably, there is little professional support for balance and for honoring, respecting, and taking responsibility for all of who we are.

Moreover, the greater value placed on intellectual achievement, technical proficiency, and skill development relegates the relationship itself to a lesser status. It becomes adjunctive to the more critical components of the job. As such, the relationship receives little attention an can easily be dismissed as superfluous and unimportant. As one professional put it, "It gets in the way. It has no dollar value." Concerned with appeasing these greater gods, we are left alarmingly ill-equipped to recognize and handle relational concerns when they occur. We therefore avoid these matters until they become large and uncontrollable and then apply solutions that eradicate the problem instead of resolving the core issues.

Furthermore, the lack of education about and professional regard for relational issues means that each of us is left alone to deal with them. The solid collegial support we so desperately need to brave the hidden dragon within becomes little more than advice to protect our flank and hide our mistakes. Rather than acting out of their concern for what we must face if we are to grow, our colleagues relate to us out of their own fear about what might happen if they were in our shoes. Indeed, in situations where we share responsibility for the violation with others, our compatriots may well divorce themselves from the incident and from their shame and leave us to hang alone. To dissociate from us, our colleagues may even gossip about our story to elevate their insider status and disqualify us professionally.

Without permission to develop all of who we are, support for tending the relationship, and help to pick ourselves up when we falter, we receive little encouragement to engage in relational healing. Wandering this desert alone is painful and requires tremendous integrity and courage.

It is no wonder that we rarely undertake this hazardous and fear-laden journey.

SOCIETAL BARRIERS

Our resistance to relational healing is buttressed by the prevailing popularity of an adversarial model of justice. More Americans are suing than ever before. The proliferation of attorneys insidiously feeds this dynamic. There are 600,000 lawyers in practice in the United States, or one for every 400 Americans, with another 40,000 graduating every year from law school (Barnard, 1991). This explosion has spawned more laws that define and protect more rights that, in turn, need to be enforced by the legal system. The current popularity and feasibility of malpractice actions are reflected in the statement of a client who said, "If my new therapist kicked me out the way my old one did, I'd sue her today."

Without casting undue aspersions on the legal profession, we need to be aware that this trend forces both clients and professionals to save themselves at the expense of the relationship. Moreover, rather than cultivating an internal process of growth, the adversarial process of resolution forces professionals to deny that we use or have used clients to meet our needs. We cannot afford to acknowledge to ourselves or to others what happened, since to do so would be an admission of guilt that could jeopardize our defense and conceivably cost us money and, perhaps, more important, our careers.

Indeed, once the legal apparatus is set in motion, the possibility of relational healing disappears. Rivalry destroys whatever is left of the connection and the goal becomes punishment of the professional, protection of the public, or compensation for damages to the client. The emphasis on winning makes for two versions of the truth and leaves no room for an apology. As a result, any hope for the professional-client relationship—both as a wounded entity or as an avenue for healing—is abandoned and the significance of the relationship loses again.

The ease with which we professionals now consider the legalistic approach is disquieting. It suggests that preserving the connection with our clients is not very important or worthy of our efforts. It is also a commentary on how deeply we deny our own personal power to mend what has been torn and how deeply we deny the power of relationship.

Another social trend that further militates against the use of a relational model for healing is quietly emerging. As the concern for clients' safety has become more distinct, boards of licensure are taking stronger measures against professionals who violate the standards of responsibility. Having been criticized for their laxness, they seek to avoid the charge of collusion and, therefore, focus on legalistic approaches rather than healing alternatives. Unfortunately, angry and vindictive clients and professionals show some tendencies to play on the paranoia of these boards, using their reactiveness as a tool for revenge.

In the real world, some boundary violations are criminal acts deserving of punishment and some professionals should be helped to move into alternative lines of work. However, with the increase in client complaints has come a new McCarthyism wherein some professionals have taken it upon themselves to search out the "bad apples" in the bunch, deeming them untouchables and beyond redemption. This witch hunt has fascistic overtones. This self-righteous and punitive attitude creates an atmosphere wherein human error is regarded as sin and the intent of colleagues is to destroy rather than to help.

Cultivating a we-they mentality within each profession is perilous for all of us. Legalism and the reactionary zealousness, punitiveness, and gossip of professionals have the effect of closing off the possibility that professionals will share with one other the mistakes they make and the very real dilemmas their fields impose. If this spirit of condemnation persists, we professionals can never risk being open to learning and growing from our mistakes. We also cannot risk healing the wounds with our clients relationally, because our attention must first go to our immediate survival. Since we, too, might find ourselves to be sinners, we avoid looking at ourselves and instead become invested in focusing our attention on the behavior of others. Undoubtedly, we need to adequately police each of our professions and confront rather than silently collude in the misconduct of our colleagues. However, we also need to carefully scrutinize our motives before we join a punitive crusade that can only destroy the possibilities for relational healing.

A WARNING ABOUT CHARACTER-DISORDERED PROFESSIONALS AND CLIENTS

It would be dangerously naive not to recognize that there are some situations where relational healing should not be tried. Three character disorders—narcissism, antisocialism, and borderline personality—come under this umbrella. Persons with these disorders lack the capacity to relate nonmanipulatively and, therefore, are not capable of engaging in authentic dialogue. More specifically, they tend to be highly egotistical and to perceive and experience all interpersonal interaction as power and control issues. Given that their primary agenda is to come out on top, any efforts to engage with them are destined to be nonproductive and probably destructive.

Professionals Who Are Character-Disordered

For professionals, taking on the role of being someone who is special and powerful allows the professional-client relationship to work. Unfortunately, this role is a magnet for the character-disordered because it fits their overblown self-image and provides them with the opportunity to take advantage of those with less power. Rather than deny their needs (which is the problem for most professionals), these individuals feel *entitled* to use clients for their own ends.

When confronted with the impact of their behavior, professionals who are narcissistic are unable to empathize and identify with the client's experience. Instead, they become even more self-centered and self-absorbed. Professionals who are antisocial cannot feel the remorse that is essential to correcting harmful behavior. Lacking a conscience, these individuals continue to use the relationship to garner more power for themselves.

Since narcissistic professionals see clients as extensions of themselves and antisocial professionals view clients as tools to be used, the self-other boundary does not exist. Unable to connect in any trustworthy way with others, character-disordered professionals can take but cannot give. Therefore, they never take real responsibility for how they affect their clients.

Clients Who Are Character-Disordered

Being made special initiates the boundary violation for many clients. For those clients who are diagnosed as having a borderline, narcissistic, or antisocial personality, being special merely feeds their disease, because it matches their grandiose self-image and makes them feel more powerful than they really are. When the harmful consequences from a violation emerge, they feel robbed and struggle to maintain their exclusive place with the professional. If and when their efforts fail, they react with rage to their feeling abandoned and try to destroy the professional. Attempts at relational healing are futile because these clients will seek to win or hurt in retaliation rather than to heal the wound. Indeed, when highly functioning professionals make themselves emotionally vulnerable, character-disordered clients take it a sign of personal weakness, which they can then use as an opportunity to gain the upper edge and to control the professional.

How to Protect Yourself

Recognizing character-disordered clients and professionals is difficult because they often cover their disease with a normal facade. By using appropriate language and eye contact, and by behaving properly, they induce us to trust their obvious presentation. Consequently, we have to focus on the covert and often intuitively subtle aspects of their behavior to assess who they really are.

Our most reliable clue may be a residual sense or impression that something did not quite fit, something was not quite right, or something did not make sense during our interaction. The difficulty in naming precisely what was wrong is common and should not be taken as an indication of mistaken judgment. The ability of these individuals to mask their intent creates an illusory situation such that what is wrong appears not in the content but rather in the process of our interacting together. Therefore, we need to trust our internal reactions and count on the greater wisdom of our intuition.

Fortunately, the vast majority of professionals and clients are not character-disordered. Thus, it is incumbent on us as professionals not to use this warning as the newest automatic excuse for avoiding relational healing. We all are vulnerable to committing boundary violations as part of our day-to-day interplay. Awareness is our best protection against normalizing these otherwise painful events. Since clients who are character-disordered are apt to initiate boundary violations, it is especially important, however, for professionals to be educated about these diseases if we are to respond effectively.

OUR LOSS OF FAITH

We have looked at ourselves, our educational and professional institutions, and our society to better understand the barriers to relational healing. We now have to face another truth about ourselves, a truth that has overwhelming implications for each of us, our clients, and the future of the professional-client relationship: Our faith is dying. We have culturally secularized, diminished, and denied the spiritual basis of the professional-client relationship. This erosion has left us numb to what we may have done or are doing to our clients. Moreover, we have little or no faith in what we and our clients, students, patients, and parishioners can do together. Our minimization of what has historically been a sacred connection has enabled many of us to invest in a competitive market focused on profit rather than service. In effect, we have changed the philosophical context in which we work while pretending that the quality of the service we offer is the same or better.

The connection between us and our clients is frayed not only at the edges but closer to the relational core. As a result, we increasingly view clients as potential enemies. Rather than holding on to our positive power to heal, nurture, and teach, we transfer and ascribe it negatively to them. Since they can hurt us, we feel compelled to defend against them rather than being mutually—though never equally—powerful in the relationship. We look first therefore to secular solutions—our codes of ethics, institutional policies, and professional standards of conduct—to handle the moral injustices between us. Rather than use them as guiding principles to preserve the health of the relationship, we use them as literal *do*'s and *don't*'s to protect ourselves. Being afraid of what our clients might do to us, we draw the boundary of safety around ourselves, become technically compliant, and quietly leave the relationship. In so doing, we shut off what we have to give, which destroys the spiritual bond between us and our clients.

As a result, our clients have less trust with which to enter the unknown with us. They turn instead to information about their consumer rights so as to be better educated and protected in their relationships with us. Granted, clients do have to be more discriminating and self-determining; however, their thrust to minimize their dependency sets them up to be co-equal and responsible in situations where they can never know as much as we do. As one client said, "I don't want an equal-opportunity surgeon. That's passing the buck. I want respect instead of abdication."

Regardless of the possibly dangerous and long-range ramifications for clients, this trend does suggest that clients are skeptical about our care and concern—qualities that are life-giving to the spiritual connection between us and them. Like us, our clients are afraid and have less hope that together we can resolve the issues between us. They turn to legalistic—and sterile—avenues to manage their pain.

If we and our clients are pitted against each other and we each scramble for our own personal safety, there is less possibility that either of us will choose or trust in a relational path toward reconciliation. Sadly, as our faith dies and we are no longer vested in each other, we embark on a final journey that ominously takes us both toward our own isolation and destruction. Destroying our faith in one other leaves us alone and unprotected. Since all of us are innately dependent creatures with core needs, we cannot survive if we are unconnected and left to fend for ourselves. Yet, as we professionals care less and our clients trust less, we together unravel the spiritual fabric that breathes life into our existence and makes our mutual survival possible.

A PLEA TO EDUCATORS

While it falls on all of us who are part of the morally and ethically based professions to become aware of and change this tragic flow of events, the mantle rests most heavily on those educators who are responsible for training professionals. Instead of responding to market demands and ignoring the erosion of the moral dimension, educators have to prepare future generations of professionals to own their power and to understand the comprehensive nature of the professional-client connection. To do so, educators will have to accept their greater responsibility to society at large and become courageous to go against those forces that currently dominate the professional landscape.

For students to emerge as accountable physicians, clerics, therapists, attorneys, or teachers, they have to be taught to be responsible to the relationship and sensitive to context. They also have to be given the tools to monitor intentionality, anticipate consequences, and recognize and regulate their impact. And these tools are accessible.

Armed with these tools, we can identify boundary violations by noting when we have reversed roles with our clients, created secrets, double-bound clients in their freedom to respond, and used our privilege to pursue our own needs. Should we commit a violation, we also have a model we can follow to help heal the wound and preserve the integrity of the relationship. Most important, we no longer have to be ignorant of our power or of the damage we may inflict on our clients.

We have the means available to prevent and mend violations; we just have to make the choice to use them. Only when we do will there be the possibility for real safety in the professional-client relationship. In the final analysis, it is not so much we or our clients who are at risk as it is the relationship between us.

REFERENCES

American Bar Association (1990). Model code of professional responsibility. In T. Morgan & R. Rotunda. *1990 Selected standards on professional responsibility*. New York: Foundation Press.

Barnard, J. (1991). America's Least Wanted. *Law and Politics, 5(11)*, 11–15.

Book of common prayer (1979). New York: Church Hymnal Corporation.

Buber, M. (1988). *The knowledge of man: Selected essays*. Atlantic Highlands, NJ: Humanities Press International.

Chodorow, N. (1978). *The reproduction of mothering: Psychoanalysis and the sociology of gender*. Berkeley, CA: University of California Press.

Covington, S. (1986). Physical, emotional and sexual abuse. *Focus on family and chemical dependency, 9*, 10–44.

Dubin, L. (1988). Sex and the divorce lawyer: Is the client off limits. *Georgetown Journal of Legal Ethics, 1*, 585–619.

Edelstein, L. (1967). *Ancient medicine*. Baltimore, MD: Johns Hopkins Press.

Eliade, M. (1964). *Shamanism: Archaic techniques of ecstasy*. Princeton: Princeton University Press.

Ethics Committee of the American Psychological Association (1988). Trends in ethics cases, common pitfalls, and published resources. *American Psychologist, 43(7)*, 564–572.

Fortune, M. (1989). Betrayal of the pastoral relationship: Sexual contact by pastors and pastoral counselors. In G. Schoener, J. Milgrom, J. Gonsiorek et al., *Psychotherapists' sexual involvement with clients*. Minneapolis, MN: Walk-In Counseling Center.

Friedman, M. (1960). *Martin Buber: The life of dialogue*. New York: Harper and Row.

Gartrell, N., Olarte, S., & Herman, J. (1986). Institutional resistance to self study: A case report. In A. Burgess & C. Hartman (Eds.), *Sexual exploitation of patients by health professionals*. New York: Praeger.

Gilligan, C. (1982). *In a different voice: Psychological theory and women's development*. Cambridge, MA: Harvard University Press.

King, S. (1987). The way of the adventurer. In S. Nicholson (Ed.), *Shamanism: An expanded view of reality*. Wheaton, IL: Theosophical Publishing House.

Kuchan, A. (1989). Survey of incidence of psychotherapists' sexual contact with clients in Wisconsin. In G. Schoener, J. Milgrom, J. Gonsiorek et al., *Psychotherapists' sexual involvement with clients*. Minneapolis, MN: Walk-In Counseling Center.

Macalester College (1988). *Macalester College 1988-90 Catalog*. St. Paul, MN: author.

Maslow, A. (1968). *Toward a psychology of being*. New York: Van Nostrand Reinhold.

National Federation of Societies for Clinical Social Work (1988). *Code of ethics*. Arlington, VA: author.

Robertson, D., Dyer, C., & Campbell, D. (1985). *Report on survey of sexual harassment policies and procedures*. (Unpublished manuscript) Bloomington, IL: Office for Women's Affairs, Indiana University.

Schoener, G. (1989). A look at the literature. In G. Schoener, J. Milgrom, J. Gonsiorek et al., *Psychotherapists' sexual involvement with clients*. Minneapolis, MN: Walk-In Counseling Center.

Sheehan, K. H., Sheehan, D. V., White, K., Leibowitz, A., & Baldwin, D. C. Jr. (1990). A pilot study of medical student abuse. Student perceptions of mistreatment and misconduct in medical school. *Journal of the American Medical Association, 263(4)*, 532–537.

Steinbrook, R. (1990). Medical students often abused. *Los Angeles Times*, January 26, 29A.

Veatch, R. (1985). The relationship of the profession(al) to society. *Journal of Dental Education, 48(4)*, 207–213.

INDEX